FRANCES LINCOLN

First published in 2022
by Frances Lincoln,
an imprint of The Quarto Group.
The Old Brewery, 6 Blundell Street
London, N7 9BH,
United Kingdom
T (0)20 7700 6700
www.Quarto.com

ISBN 978-0-7112-5973-7
Ebook ISBN 978-0-7112-5974-4

10 9 8 7 6 5 4 3 2 1

Design by Sarah Boris
Printed in China

MIX
Paper from
responsible sources
FSC® C016973

ROBERT DIMERY

MUSIC

QUAKE

THE MOST DISRUPTIVE MOMENTS IN MUSIC

INTRODUCTION

Who's this? Answer on p.184

The whole premise of this book is the overturning of expectations. Sometimes that goes hand in hand with uproar – a concert-hall riot, say, or the outcry at an uncomfortable lyric, or plain disbelief at what is being presented as 'music'. But the 50 explosive moments covered here pushed the art form forwards, redefined and renewed it, whether it was appreciated at the time or only later.

Such moments don't spring forth fully formed out of a vacuum. Igor Stravinsky's 1913 score for the ballet *The Rite of Spring* borrowed from traditional folk songs, not least in its jarring rhythms. And by around 1910, Arnold Schoenberg was well on his way to instigating the most radical shake-up in musical theory for centuries, but had once composed in the Late Romantic style and was influenced (and championed) by Gustav Mahler.

Many of these turning points were made possible by advances in technology, and we'll look at these in tandem. The change from analogue recording, onto cylinders or primitive disks, to electronic recording in the 1920s boosted audio clarity – important when a soloist is making history. (Louis Armstrong's Hot Five and Hot Seven studio sessions straddled the change-over.) The introduction of microphones allowed for greater subtlety and nuance in a vocal performance; magnetic tape laid the ground for multitracking.

This book also examines how technological innovation can bring about unexpected shifts in the zeitgeist – witness the ructions Napster wrought and the threats to the hegemony of the music industry. And when it's 'mis-used', technology can open doors we weren't aware were even there: sound recordings slowed down, cut up and edited by the likes of Pierre Schaeffer, Steve Reich or Tom Moulton (all discussed in the book) become orphaned from their original context, alien and intriguing. In the Bronx sometime in the 1970s, inspired DJs evolved new sonic possibilities by 'scratching' with vinyl records. And the ready availability of budget samplers such as the Akai MPC series in the late 1980s further transformed music-making, enabling untrained musicians to collage together snippets from existing recordings, a breakthrough that forged the iconic textures of old-school hip-hop sound.

In the 1960s, forward-thinking minds found new and thrilling ways of 'mis-using' recording studios too, repurposing them from a means of faithfully recording live performance into an Aladdin's Cave for creating new aural worlds that couldn't be reproduced on stage. You can hear this in the extraordinary sound palettes dreamed up by technically savvy, maverick spirits such as the British producer Joe Meek, Daphne Oram, who founded the BBC Radiophonic Workshop, and Delia Derbyshire, who worked there.

Exceptional female creatives such as Derbyshire often found their innovations underappreciated, and her role in the evolution of electronic sound was acknowledged only in retrospect. A microcosm of historical injustice right there: 'Women are the glue,' Björk told *Pitchfork* in 2015. 'It's invisible, what women do.' Flick through this book and you'll notice that some of its most uncompromising artistic statements were made by women, from Billie Holiday's 'Strange Fruit' (1939) through Brigitte Fontaine's *Comme à la Radio* (1969) and Patti Smith's *Horses* (1975) to the Slits' *Cut* (1979). Over the last 50 years, few artists have been as daringly innovative, while operating within pop's parameters, as Kate Bush and Björk. Today, the balance is somewhat redressed with the bold statements (musical and otherwise) of formidable female artists such as Beyoncé – a pop-culture deity who introduced a socio-political edge to what was already a stellar career, and added a new dimension to her art in the process.

As Jimi Hendrix permanently changed perceptions of what a guitar could do, so others altered the fabric of music so radically that the reverberations of their legacy endured for years, some still resonating today. John Cage questioned musical conventions rigorously, engineering new tonalities for the piano and upturning accepted ideas of what constitutes 'music'. Kraftwerk's retrofuturistic synth pop influenced such disparate artists as David Bowie and Brian Eno (who was also deeply indebted to Cage's radical artistic philosophy), Bronx hip-hoppers Afrika Bambaataa and the fledgling Run-DMC, pioneers of Detroit techno including Derrick May and Juan Atkins, and Daft Punk, who themselves reshaped dance music at the turn of the 21st century.

You'll also discover how a stimulating cross-pollination of ideas makes for unlikely kindred spirits. Stravinsky's development of a new rhythmic language – involving syncopation and unexpected accents – as well as harmonic innovations in *The Rite of Spring* resonated warmly with jazz musicians. Charlie Parker assimilated the opening notes of the *Rite* into his solo on 'Salt Peanuts' during a performance in Paris in 1949, and delighted the composer when (without acknowledging his presence) he dropped the opening notes of Stravinsky's 1910 suite *The Firebird* into the second chorus of his song 'Ko-Ko' at Manhattan's Birdland Jazz Club.

Karlheinz Stockhausen's interest in producing sounds from unorthodox sources – and blending electronically generated sonics with acoustic ones – famously impacted on the Beatles' Paul McCartney (for whom *Gesang der Jünglinge* was 'my big favourite plick-plop piece of his'). And Stockhausen peers out from the cover of their 1967 opus *Sgt. Pepper's Lonely Hearts Club Band*, a brooding face behind the shoulder of comedian W.C. Fields. That marriage of avant-garde risk-taking with a pop sensibility characterizes some of the most influential works discussed here, from the Velvet Underground & Nico's debut album (1967) to Jimi Hendrix's scorching reinterpretation of the US national anthem (1969), the dizzying production games on Missy Elliott's ground-breaking *Supa Dupa Fly* (1997) or Radiohead's wrong-footing *Kid A* (2000).

Most of these pivotal 50 events are recordings, although there's space too for a handful of extraordinary live performances that caused quakes of their own. You'll also find a series of features running through the book as a complement to the main entries, offering further insight into them, or into a related area. Part of this commentary involves tracing the revolution in the way we listen to music, and how this has affected music-makers. Among the issues this throws up is the role of the album in the 21st century – whether it still has relevance, how its format has evolved to include visual complements, and how artists have experimented with the process of an album release.

Think of this book as a tale of 50 phoenixes, rising blazingly new from the ashes of the everyday: 50 fifth columnists within pop's castle; 50 windows into the future.

Opposite: At the zenith of the hippie era, Woodstock festival saw some 400,000 free spirits descend on a dairy farm in New York State

WOODSTOCK
MUSIC & ART FAIR
presents
AN
AQUARIAN
EXPOSITION
in
WHITE LAKE, N.Y.
woodstock
a Film by MICHAEL WADLEIGH
Produced by BOB MAURICE
AUGUST
15, 16, 17.
3 DAYS
of PEACE
& MUSIC

THIS IS
THE MODERN
WORLD

1913–1953

The early 20th century saw social tumult and a redrawing of national borders, but also astounding cross-cultural innovation and invention. The political map had become increasingly fluid in the preceding century, with the unification of Germany in 1871, a rash of annexations and land grabs by colony-hungry European powers, assassinations and the rise of anarchism. That global instability led to the 1914–18 'War to End all Wars', when mechanized warfare drove the death toll to around 8.5 million. The onerous reparations placed on the defeated Germany stoked resentment within the country.

Instability and change became the watchwords. In *The Interpretation of Dreams* (1899) and *The Psychopathology of Everyday Life* (1901), Sigmund Freud unveiled a secret world of hidden motivations and psychoneurosis within us all. Albert Einstein's 1905 and 1915 papers challenged established concepts of space and time. And by the 1920s, scientists including Max Planck, Niels Bohr, Erwin Schrödinger, Werner Heisenberg and Max Born had begun mapping out quantum theory, substituting iron-clad certainties of classical mechanics with more nebulous concepts.

Inevitably, the seismic repercussions of such events, and their impact on the human sensibilities, were echoed in the arts. Expressionism and Fauvism used vibrant colour to map inner emotions; Cubism fractured its subject matter, presenting multiple views simultaneously; Dadaism and Surrealism employed irrationality to mock the bourgeois, capitalist societies that had birthed World War I. In literature, Modernist writers including James Joyce, T.S. Eliot, William Faulkner and Virginia Woolf evolved radical new prose to express the non-linear flurry of thought and existence.

An entirely new art form – cinema – developed with exponential speed, from silent-screen landmarks such as Georges Méliès's *A Trip to the Moon* (1902) and D.W. Griffith's controversial epic *The Birth of a Nation* (1915), to the first 'talkie' (*The Jazz Singer*, 1927) and the heydays of German Expressionism, Film Noir and Italian Neorealism.

All of this artistic change inevitably filtered into music. Pioneering composers such as Richard Wagner, Richard Strauss and Claude Debussy had already composed tonally ambiguous works, and drawn on non-Western influences in their compositions. Arnold Schoenberg and his disciples went further, creating daringly challenging works shorn of the musical signposts (recognizable overall structure, melodic development, harmonic resolution) with which audiences were familiar. In turn, and in tandem with parallel alterations from the likes of later innovators including John Cage, such modernizations questioned accepted ideas of what constituted 'music'. In the USA, imported European traditions were now challenged by home-grown musical forces such as jazz and the blues.

Initially decried for its supposed degeneracy, jazz soundtracked the 'Roaring 20s' in America, a period of euphoria for a fortunate few ('Something had to be done with all the nervous energy stored up and unexpended in the War,' observed

F. Scott Fitzgerald wryly) that saw increasing national wealth and skyrocketing shares. But the global stock market crashes in 1929 foreshadowed mass unemployment and the Great Depression of the 1930s. In Weimar Republic-era Germany, hyperinflation reached such a pitch that an item in a shop window might rise in price in the time it took to step inside.

Into the vacuum rushed Adolf Hitler and his vision of a triumphant Third Reich, though his defeat in the global 1939–45 war also cost Britain dearly in terms of debt. Its unwieldly empire – encompassing around a quarter of the world's population – entered slow decline, and the violent severing of its 'jewel', India, prompted a string of further secessions, domino-like. By the start of the 1950s, the USA and the Soviet Union were the last superpowers standing, poised on the brink of another war, although one less clearly defined than before.

'MAKE IT NEW.'

EZRA POUND

1914
→ The assassination of Archduke Franz-Ferdinand in Bosnia and Herzegovina (Sarajevo) becomes the catalyst for World War I.

1915
→ D.W. Griffith directs the controversial epic *The Birth of a Nation.*

1917
→ 'Livery Stable Blues', by the Original Dixieland 'Jass' Band, is the first jazz record.

1919
→ Walter Gropius inaugurates the influential design school Bauhaus in Weimar.

1920
→ Women gain full voting rights in the USA.

1922
→ In a high-water year for modernist literature, James Joyce's daringly innovative but controversial novel *Ulysses* is published in France.

1923
→ Arnold Schoenberg's 'Suite for Piano' is the first of his 12-tone compositions.

1925
→ Major US record labels adopt the new 'electric' system of recording (including microphones, amplifiers and machinery) developed by Western Electrics, greatly improving audio fidelity and dynamic range on recordings.

1927
→ Warner Brothers' *The Jazz Singer* heralds the demise of silent cinema and the birth of the 'talkies'.

1928
→ Premiere of Walt Disney's animated short *Steamboat Willie*, marking the first appearance of Mickey Mouse.

1929
→ The Wall Street stock market crash in New York presages a global economic recession dubbed the Great Depression.

1935

→ George Gershwin's musical *Porgy and Bess* – based on Black folk genres, notably jazz and spiritual music – premieres with a cast consisting of actors of colour.

1937

→ In Germany, the Nazi Party stages an exhibition entitled '*Entartete Kunst*' ('Degenerate Art') to highlight so-called undesirable features of contemporary art.

1939

→ Germany's invasion of Poland on 1 September prompts a declaration of war by Great Britain and France, leading to the onset of World War II.

1941

→ Japanese forces bomb Pearl Harbor in Hawaii, leading to the USA's entry into World War II.
→ Premiere of Orson Welles's *Citizen Kane*.

1942

→ Bing Crosby's version of 'White Christmas' is released. Penned by Irving Berlin, it will become the bestselling single of all time.

1945

→ 'Trinity', the first nuclear bomb test, is staged in the New Mexico desert, marking the culmination of the Manhattan Project.
→ US forces drop two atomic bombs over the Japanese cities of Hiroshima and Nagasaki, effectively ending World War II.

1948

→ South Africa's government instigates apartheid.

1949

→ Publication of George Orwell's *1984*.

1953

→ Francis Crick and James Watson discover DNA's double helix.

A BEAST AMONG THE BEAU MONDE

PREMIERE OF *THE RITE OF SPRING*
COMPOSER: IGOR STRAVINSKY
CHOREOGRAPHER: VASLAV NIJINSKY
1913

The opening night of the ballet *The Rite of Spring* on 29 May 1913 at Paris's Théâtre des Champs-Elysées embodies the shock of the new in all its raw audacity. The startling score and radical choreography provoked jeers, sarcastic applause and (allegedly) at least one duel the following day. Urbane German diplomat Count Harry Kessler recorded the event in his diary as 'A thoroughly new vision . . . a new kind of wildness, both un-art and art . . . All forms laid waste and new ones emerging suddenly from the chaos.'

The roots of this scandal of scandals date from three years before, and an unsettling dream: Igor Stravinsky's vision of a young girl dancing herself to death, encircled by tribal elders, in a heathen ritual to appease the god of spring (its original title was 'The Great Sacrifice'). The same year, the composer had enjoyed a giddily rapid rise to fame with his ballet *The Firebird*, a success that would be resoundingly followed up with *Petrushka* (1911); as with the *Rite*, both ballets were commissioned by Ballets Russes impresario Serge Diaghilev. The seeds of what was to come were already there. Jerkily syncopated accents dot *Firebird*'s 'Infernal Dance', along with a highly chromatic palette. *Petrushka* ramps up the rhythmic complexity still further, adding passages of polytonality in which different musical keys occur simultaneously. But those works were immediately and rapturously acclaimed.

The *Rite* was a darker beast, harder to love. Its musical motifs drew heavily on Russian peasant music, including folk-song collections orchestrated by his former teacher, Nikolai Rimsky-Korsakov, as well as wedding songs from Lithuania. But Stravinsky refashioned those paysan melodies as his contemporaries Georges Braque and Pablo Picasso might have pieced together a Cubist collage. Musicians were asked to play outside their instruments' usual range (witness the high, strained opening motif on bassoon), while Stravinsky amassed the forces of the largest orchestra he'd ever write for, creating a musical powerhouse. Major and minor triads (three-note chords) were gratingly piled on top of each other; time signatures changed with unnerving speed. Most daring of all were Stravinsky's rhythmic innovations, thrillingly heard in 'The Augurs of Spring', in which shifting accents and syncopation aggressively blindside the listener, and 'Procession of the Sage', in which different instruments, playing in unison, are allotted separate rhythmic patterns (eccentric meters were common to Russian folk music, but Stravinsky

Costumier Yann Seabra's designs for the *Rite* reflected the folkloric inspirations of Stravinsky's score

'IT HAS NO RELATION TO MUSIC AT ALL AS MOST OF US UNDERSTAND THE WORD.'

MUSICAL TIMES

switched them with breath-taking speed). All of which admirably served the brutality and pagan otherness at the heart of the *Rite*.

And seasoned Parisian ballet-goers would have seen nothing like Nijinsky's choreography. To suggest heathen ungainliness, he had his dancers land flat (and painfully) on their feet after leaps and turn their toes inwards. The troupe stamped and jerked in primordial awkwardness, rather than soaring skywards or poising elegantly *en pointe*; an unthinking mass blindly playing out their role.

Stravinsky's ballet married the prehistorically ancient to the avant-garde modern. Writing in 1921, the poet T.S. Eliot felt it transfigured 'the rhythm of the steppes into the scream of the motor horn, the rattle of machinery, the grind of wheels, the beating of iron and steel, the roar of the underground railway, and the other barbaric cries of modern life'.

The score unquestionably wrongfooted and even angered critics. 'It has no relation to music at all as most of us understand the word,' sniffed London's *Musical Times* after the *Rite* opened there later that year. The audience at the world premiere was a combustible mixture of aristocracy, bourgeoisie, the *demimonde* and progressive aesthetes, but it's a moot point as to whether the consternation represented a spontaneous outburst of feelings. One of the dancers, Lydia Sokolova, felt that 'They had got themselves all ready. They didn't even let the music be played for the overture.' Nijinsky's choreography for Debussy's ballet *Jeux*, premiered a fortnight previously, had attracted critical brickbats, which doubtless carried over, while the volume of the fracas made it almost impossible for the dancers to coordinate with the orchestra. But tellingly, it seems the term 'riot' wasn't attached to the *Rite* until 1924, and then in connection with a performance at Carnegie Hall. Indeed, impassioned applause rang out at the end of the Paris premiere, with Stravinsky and Nijinsky taking several curtain calls. And all concerned would certainly have been alive to the publicity value of a good controversy.

For some five years, Arnold Schoenberg had been evolving a form of music unshackled to conventional harmony or development; the last of his *Three Pieces for Piano* (1909) may represent the earliest 'atonal' composition – one with no clear key. Anton Webern and Alban Berg, two of his pupils, keenly followed suit and the three became the highest-profile members of what was dubbed the 'Second Viennese School' (the 'First' being that of Mozart, Beethoven and Haydn).

On 31 March 1913 in Vienna, Schoenberg was scheduled to conduct his *Chamber Symphony No.1*, Webern's *Six Pieces for Orchestra* and two of Berg's *Five Orchestral Songs after Postcards by Peter Altenberg*. But the dissonance of Berg's composition (the wind section sounds 12 different pitches simultaneously at one point) and Altenberg's heavily sexual poetry unleashed violent confrontation. Unlike the *Rite*, the concert was abandoned.

Schoenberg retreated to hone his version of the '12-tone' system (also known as serialism), which constructed a guiding principle for composition based on manipulating a fixed series (or 'row') of all 12 notes in an octave. Berg and Webern were, if anything, more committed to this vision than Schoenberg. Berg's opera *Wozzeck* (1921) was starkly atonal, though his instrumental *Lyric Suite* (1925–26) had a beauty and stillness that gave serialism a more welcoming face.

Webern's compositions were exquisitely concise (his 1928 symphony lasted just 10 minutes) and veered violently between dynamic extremes, expanding the 12-tone method to incorporate aspects of musical performance such as pitch, timbre, articulation and even the length of silences. In mapping out the musical building blocks so rigorously, he created a template that would be put to provocative use by such *enfants terribles* as Karlheinz Stockhausen and Pierre Boulez and their explorations into 'total serialism'.

THE BIRTH OF AMERICAN CONCERT MUSIC

RHAPSODY IN BLUE
GEORGE GERSHWIN
1924

By 1924, Gershwin and his brother Ira had penned five years' worth of sophisticated pop hits. But he also had ambitions to create long-form piece inspired by America's native jazz and blues. So when bandleader Paul Whiteman asked him to write such a work for his concert 'An Experiment in Modern Music' at New York's Aeolian Hall on 12 February 1924, Gershwin jumped at the chance.

Whiteman's well-meaning ambition was to add a sheen of respectability to jazz, then vilified for its suggestive, syncopated rhythms and low origins in New Orleans's bars and bordellos.

Rhapsody in Blue perfectly realized the goals of both musicians. As a joke in rehearsal, Whiteman's clarinettist Ross Gorman had improvised the striking opening glissando; Gershwin kept it, and that wailing prelude stopped the Aeolian's largely listless audience in its tracks. Bluesy seventh notes pepper the melody, which becomes the main theme, sometimes as blocks of pounding chords that recall the pianism of Sergei Rachmaninoff (seated in the audience that night). A tight deadline had forced Gershwin to dip into his musical leftovers, which he strung together with original compositions. No meaningful thematic development then (as critics disparagingly noted), but the jazz-flavoured bluesy harmonies, call-and-response elements and improvisatory excursions provide continuity. The *Rhapsody*'s ecstatic reception on the night announced a new musical form – symphonic jazz – while its extended structure influenced Duke Ellington's 'Creole Rhapsody' (1931), among others.

Later, Gershwin revealed that his inspiration for the work began with the rackety rhythms of a train he was riding on, and he conceived *Rhapsody* as 'a sort of musical kaleidoscope of America, of our vast melting pot, of our unduplicated national pep, of our metropolitan madness'. Like Edgard Varèse's rawer *Amériques* (1918–21), the *Rhapsody* is a response to the majesty and madness of New York City, the definitive modern metropolis and epicentre of the Jazz Age.

But *Rhapsody in Blue* also explored tantalizing new ground for the genre, a bold New World art music at a time when most American composers were still in thrall to the traditions of the Old World and studied there. 'Music must reflect the thoughts and aspirations of the people and the time,' Gershwin insisted. 'My people are Americans. My time is today.'

A sheet-music transcription of the work that dressed the bawdy upstart jazz in highbrow classical duds

JAZZ'S TEN COMMANDMENTS

HOT FIVE AND HOT SEVEN SESSIONS
LOUIS ARMSTRONG
1925–29

Born in late 19th-century New Orleans, jazz was a gumbo seasoned with ragtime, blues, brass marching bands, minstrelsy and more. It drew heavily on African musical traditions: improvisation, call-and-response chants, simultaneous cross-rhythms, syncopation. The first titan of jazz, Louis Armstrong learned to play cornet in one of the city's reform schools, where he was sent in 1913. In 1918 – still a teenager but already a head-turning musician – he replaced his early mentor Joe 'King' Oliver as cornetist in Edward 'Kid' Ory's band. Four years later he was playing second cornet with Oliver's Creole Jazz Band in Chicago, and in 1924 he joined Fletcher Henderson's orchestra in New York. Sometimes uncredited, Armstrong lit up a string of the era's bestselling sides, from Henderson's 'Sugar Foot Stomp' to Bessie Smith's epochal 'The St Louis Blues'.

Chicago's OKeh Records took note, signing him in autumn 1925. Having swiftly assembled a quartet – his second wife Lil on piano, alongside Kid Ory (trombone), Johnny St Cyr (banjo) and Johnny Dodds (clarinet) – and with scant rehearsal, Armstrong kicked off recording on 12 November.

The tracks laid down by his ensembles over the next four years would remake jazz, opening up possibilities that every successive generation, knowingly or not, continues to explore. Louis Armstrong turned jazz into a platform for virtuoso soloists, jettisoning the anchors of a song's original melody for displays of ecstatic, freewheeling improvisation – remarkable, beautifully phrased, with a narrative-like structure and its own momentum – that dart fluidly around the beat. Notes come earlier or later than expected, on the 'weaker' second or fourth beats of a four-beat bar, injecting new pulses to the rhythm and in doing so preparing the ground for the following decade's swing music.

Take the last tune made on 12 November: 'Gut Bucket Blues', a slice of classic New Orleans ensemble playing. At the time, jazz combos worked by collective improvisation, creating a polyphony of interweaving, contrapuntal lines. Armstrong introduces the band one by one with raucous ebullience before pealing off a solo that, like a skimming stone, alights on the melody only intermittently. It proved a harbinger of more radical departures to come: his solos in 'Cornet Chop Suey' (recorded on 26 February 1926) employ tricksy syncopation and rapid-fire triplets that anticipate bebop, while unconventionally drawing on even the deepest register of his horn. (He would soon move on to the more brighter-sounding trumpet.)

Louis Armstrong's Hot Five, Exclusive Okeh Record Artists.

The Hot Five in 1925. Left to right: Louis Armstrong, Johnny St Cyr, Johnny Dodds, Kid Ory and Lil Hardin Armstrong

The same day, the quintet laid down 'Heebie Jeebies', highlighted by Armstrong's wordless 'scat' singing – today as synonymous with him as his playing. By ditching the shackles of lyrics and their attendant meaning, scatting offered new possibilities for self-expression, enabling vocalists to improvise as freely as any other musician. Scat crops up in earlier releases by Gene Greene, Fletcher Henderson and others, but none matched the sales of 'Heebie Jeebies' (it made the Hot Five the nation's most famous jazzers, although they remained a studio unit). Its success established modern scat's template and Armstrong as its prime practitioner. Through him, singers from Bing Crosby to Billie Holiday, Ella Fitzgerald and Dizzy Gillespie began scatting, while the style would adapt smoothly to bebop and even free jazz.

With an amended line-up, and now featuring tuba and drums, Armstrong's Hot Seven convened for a week in May 1927 and pushed the envelope again. His joyous second solo on 'Potato Head Blues' offers scintillating improvisation, although his tone remains characteristically rounded and clear (a contrast to his raspy scats), the notes ending in a shiver. He opens the otherwise contemplative 'West End Blues' (recorded in June 1928 with a revised Hot Five) with a startling fanfare in free time, and kicks off the final chorus with a high B-flat that builds tension that he releases with an ecstatic flurry of notes above and beyond both the rest of the ensemble and the tempo.

The Hot Five and Hot Seven cut some 90 recordings in four years. The greatest of them are as audacious in their way as Stravinsky's *The Rite of Spring* or Joyce's *Ulysses*: deconstructing the past to build new forms on its foundations. In them, you can hear the emergence of a fresh consciousness in jazz, an avant-garde break with its New Orleans origins to create something absolutely modern, an art form fitting for a young century brimming with change.

And towering over them is jazz's first great soloist.

'YOU CAN'T PLAY NOTHING ON TRUMPET THAT DOESN'T COME FROM HIM.'

MILES DAVIS

Josephine Baker performs
the Charleston in 1926 at
Paris's Folies Bergère

From 17 January 1920, the Volstead Act made the sale of
'intoxicating liquors' illegal in the United States. Prohibition
proved the mother of invention, however, as bootleggers and
speakeasies sprang up to slake the nation's thirst. And in those
drinking dens, jazz was the music of choice.

Gramophone records accelerated the rise of artists such
as Fletcher Henderson and his band (featuring Louis Armstrong)
and Duke Ellington, and white counterparts including Paul
Whiteman and Bix Beiderbecke. The 'Harlem Renaissance' saw
a cross-cultural flowering of talent, from Ellington's sophisticated
big-band innovations to inventive choreography from the likes of
Alvin Ailey (the acrobatic Lindy Hoppers date from this era),
while Josephine Baker's vivacious cabaret performances made
her a star in racially tolerant Paris. The anthology *The New
Negro* – including contributions from Zora Neale Hurston and
Langston Hughes (who evolved 'jazz poetry') – spotlighted the
strength and breadth of contemporary Black writing.

Flapper girls epitomized the era's giddy thrill. Modish and
sexually liberated, their short, drop-waisted skirts, bobbed hair
and androgynous frames marked them out from the corseted
Edwardians. F. Scott Fitzgerald captured the flamboyant times
in a string of celebrated short stories, which were undercut
with darker notes.

The 20s roared and between 1920 and 1929 America's
wealth more than doubled. But in October 1929 came the Wall
Street Crash. Soup kitchens and mass unemployment marked
the hangover after those champagne times.

A PROTEST SONG TO CHILL THE BLOOD

'STRANGE FRUIT'
BILLIE HOLIDAY
1939

On 7 August 1930, a lynch mob broke into a jail in Marion, Indiana, ejected two Black teens and hanged them in the town centre. Lawrence Beitler, a local photographer, captured the aftermath, a crowd of citizens – some smiling, one pointing – milling below the battered bodies.

Seven years later, Bronx schoolteacher Abel Meeropol was stopped in his tracks by the image; he translated his shock into a poem (which he later set to music) initially titled 'Bitter Fruit', the full meaning of which dawns slowly over the listener across three verses: Southern trees and their crop of corpses. Retitled 'Strange Fruit', it was sung by Laura Duncan at Madison Square Garden in 1938. Accounts vary as to how it made it to Billie Holiday, then performing at New York's Café Society nightclub, but she took it on, reworking it with Sonny White, her pianist, and arranger Danny Mendelsohn. For added drama (were it needed), she performed it under a spotlight in the otherwise pitch-black room, in strict silence, with waiter service paused. The audience had no choice but to face the horror. There had been earlier civil rights protest songs, but none more explicit, nor more terrifying. It closed her performance; nothing could follow it.

Holiday recorded it on 20 April 1939, a mournful but understated reading – over a funereal setting of piano and brass – that lets Meeropol's poem speak for itself. Baulking at the sensitive subject matter, her label, Columbia, passed on the track, and it was released on the independent Commodore. Radio stations – fearful of public unrest – banned it Stateside and abroad; club owners asked Holiday to drop it from her set; she was heckled. Yet despite all that, 'Strange Fruit' was a *Billboard* No.16 hit. Indeed, with million-plus sales, it became the biggest of Holiday's career, her signature piece.

And her downfall. Harry Anslinger, the zealous commissioner of the Federal Bureau of Narcotics, asked Holiday to drop the contentious song. She refused, and he targeted her as a result. In 1947, at her commercial peak, he had Holiday (a heroin user) busted and jailed for a year. Thereafter he persecuted her, quite literally, to her deathbed.

Sixty years later, *TIME* magazine declared 'Strange Fruit' the Song of the Century. Its resonance lives on in the era of Black Lives Matter and the divisive legacy of the Trump presidency, with race-related violence still all too familiar in Holiday's homeland.

'When I sing it, it affects me so much I get sick,' Holiday revealed in her autobiography, *Lady Sings the Blues*, 'It takes all the strength out of me.'

THIS IS THE MODERN WORLD 1913–1953

'I AIN'T GOT NO HOME IN THIS WORLD ANYMORE'

DUST BOWL BALLADS
WOODY GUTHRIE
1940

In the 1930s, the prairie states of America's Midwest suffered prolonged and severe droughts, turning what was once rich farmland to dust. This situation was exacerbated by intensive agricultural practices, as – prompted by demand for wheat during World War I – farmers ploughed up grassland that had held soil together.

Many fled to California, but the ravages of the Great Depression were rife there too, and the 'Okies' – as the migrants were ubiquitously dubbed – met with derision and hostility. Photographer Dorothea Lange documented their desperate plight; John Steinbeck's *Grapes of Wrath* (1939) told of it through the story of one family, the Joads; and Woody Guthrie sang about it on *Dust Bowl Ballads*.

Each track puts a human face to the hardship. 'Blowin' Down this Road' blends starry-eyed dreams of a new life of plenty in California with straight-talking demands for fair pay and treatment, though as 'Do Re Mi' advises, those without money won't be welcome in the Sunshine State and might as well stay put. The protagonist of 'Dust Cain't Kill Me' has lost everything and everyone but remains trenchantly defiant, while 'Dust Pneumonia Blues' focuses on life-shortening lung disease – including the gallows humour that the song would have yodelling but for the rattle in the singer's chest. It was standard folk singer practice to set new lyrics to old tunes, but with 'I Ain't Got No Home' Guthrie had an ulterior motive: to satirize the source gospel song, which advocated passive acceptance of hardship and deprivation with the promise of salvation in heaven. Guthrie – a native Oklahoman himself – wanted deliverance in the here and now. The two-part 'Tom Joad' tells the story of a central character in Steinbeck's novel, while another – Preacher Casey – turns up in the closer, 'Vigilante Man', to describe the armed gangs that attacked and drove away some of his fellow migrants.

Guthrie's first commercial recording, *Dust Bowl Ballads* was a landmark folk statement about a national outrage. As a collection of songs unified by one coherent theme, it also has a strong claim to being the earliest concept album, well ahead of contenders such as Frank Sinatra's *In the Wee Small Hours* (1955), where heartbreak is the connecting thread. And Guthrie's messages about hard-won truths, loss and defiance more than retain their relevance in a 21st century in which climate change and war zones spawn refugees with disheartening regularity, and armed militia groups stalk the USA–Mexico border.

An Oklahoman farmer and his sons cross a dust-blasted prospect in this Arthur Rothstein photo from 1936

INNOVATIONS IN RECORDS AND RECORDING

Studio recording was still in its infancy when Louis Armstrong cut his first Hot Five sessions for OKeh in 1925. The band played into conical horns that focused sound waves onto a diaphragm connected to a stylus that scratched a rendering onto recording cylinders, eventually superseded by discs; these acted as the master. The results were lo-fi, dynamically limited and quiet. Later that year, US studios upgraded to 'electric' systems, using microphones, signal amplifiers and recorders, greatly improving audio fidelity.

By the early 1920s, radio stations were up and running in several countries, including France, the UK, Argentina and Canada. In 1922, Americans spent $60 million on radios according to historian and editor of *Harper's* magazine, Frederick Lewis Allen. (By 1929, that figure had grown to $842,548,000 – a rise of 1,400 per cent!) Radio vastly enlarged the audience for recordings, playing a key role in spreading the enthusiasm for jazz country-wide.

World War II created an extra impetus for technological advances, accelerating the development of equipment that would, in time, be adapted for recording studios, such as equalizers, compressors and – crucially – magnetic tape. This created unlikely bedfellows. Adolf Hitler took to reel-to-reel recorders, as it allowed one of his broadcasts to be heard in one place while he was elsewhere. But singer Bing Crosby liked the idea too, relishing the prospect of pre-recording his much-loved Kraft Music Hall radio shows rather than having to perform each one live.

In 1949, Crosby presented musician and inventor Les Paul with one of the earliest Ampex reel-to-reel tape recorders. Paul discovered that by adding another playback head, he could record multiple parts ('sound-on-sound', or overdubbing) on the same tape. He and his wife Mary were able to record several guitar parts alongside layered vocals, resulting in ground-breaking hit singles such as 'How High the Moon', a US No.1 for nine weeks in 1951. Now studio recordings could be much more than simply the document of a live performance.

Les Paul at work in his LA garage-cum-studio

CBS introduced the first vinyl 10-inch and 12-inch 33⅓ LPs in 1948, although shellac 78 rpm records remained popular. Their death knell arrived with the first vinyl 7-inch singles, released by RCA Victor on 31 March 1949. Each was allotted a different coloured vinyl – decades before punk – according to genre. Among the children's songs, folk and classical offerings was Arthur 'Big Boy' Crudup's 'That's All Right', which, overhauled by Elvis Presley, would help found rock'n'roll.

Cheaper and more durable than 78s, the new format found a ready market in US teenagers in the 1950s and helped drive the popularity of juke boxes and lighter, portable record players such as the UK's Dansette, first produced in 1952.

BIRTH OF THE BOP

'KO KO'
CHARLIE PARKER
1945

**The start: a puzzle that had perplexed jazz musicians since the late 1930s.
The end: musical revolution.**

British bandleader Ray Noble wrote 'Cherokee' (1938) as part of a projected
five-movement Native Indian-themed suite; the following year, Charlie Barnet
and His Orchestra took it to No.15 on *Billboard*'s pop charts and it began cropping
up in jam sessions at New York's after-hours clubs. 'Cherokee' had a 64-bar
'AABA' structure, but whereas the opening melody was simple enough, the bridge
'B' section was another matter: difficult key changes, a lengthy chord sequence
and rapid tempo made it fiendishly difficult to nail.

Charlie 'Bird' Parker, a prodigiously talented alto saxophonist, had moved
to New York from Kansas City in 1939 and was brimful of ambition, not least to
develop a new musical vocabulary. He found the harmonies then commonplace
in jazz hackneyed, with soloists restricting themselves to playing only the notes
within a major or minor key: 'I kept thinking there's bound to be something else,'
he later reflected. 'I could hear it sometimes but I couldn't play it.'

According to Parker himself, the solution came in December that year during
a jam on 'Cherokee' in a chilli house on Seventh Avenue, when it dawned on him
that he could use any of the 12 notes in a chromatic scale – for example, every
note from C to the C above on a piano keyboard – as a melodic launch pad into
any other key. By using the upper intervals of a chord (such as the 9th, 11th or
13th) as well as the more common 1st, 3rd, 5th and 7th, he could radically
reharmonize popular standards.

The world had to wait to hear it, though. A Musicians' Union ban on all new
recordings between 1942 and 1944 – a wartime stricture to save on shellac
– prevented the nascent bebop that Parker, Thelonious Monk and others were
developing at the time from reaching a wider audience. The tune that embodied
Parker's revelations was finally recorded at his first studio session as a
bandleader – perhaps the earliest bebop recordings – on 26 November 1945,
for the Savoy label.

His sidemen included drummer Max Roach, bassist Curley Russell and
trumpeters Dizzy Gillespie and Miles Davis, but – appropriately enough for a gig
frequently dubbed the greatest jazz session ever – mystery still surrounds who
played on what. According to Davis himself, he ceded the ground to Gillespie:
'I didn't really think I was ready to play tunes at the tempo of "Cherokee" and
I didn't make no bones about it,' he recalled in his autobiography.

Bird in flight

THIS IS THE MODERN WORLD 1913–1953

In fact, a first take was reportedly cut short by the producer, Teddy Reig, once he heard the 'Cherokee' theme: Savoy's owner Herman Lubinsky was also present, and both men knew that incorporating Ray Noble's theme would mean he'd be entitled to composer's royalties. Parker was told to cut it.

The next take was the master. It kicks off with a sax/trumpet duet, reprised at the song's coda; in-between is Parker's solo – announced with a bang from Max Roach's drums, like a door thrown open to a new world – spread over two 64-bar choruses and based on the 'Cherokee' harmonies. Retitled 'Ko Ko', it streaks away at 300 beats per minute, a most dance-unfriendly pace. (Techno may hit the 160 bpm mark; drum and bass nearer 180 bpm.) Yet every note in Parker's urgent, asymmetric volley is fully articulated, vibrato-free and clear. You can't hum them, but these are melodic solos ('Playing clean and hitting the pretty notes,' in his own words) – although it requires our active participation and repeated listens to trace their lines. And the unusual way Parker accents those notes makes his phrases sound fresh to the ear. The fluid ease with which he switches between keys at high speed came from hard years of 'woodshedding' (the act of rehearsing repeatedly) demanding music, but also from the competitive 'cutting contests' he'd played at in the 1930s back in Kansas City.

Less than three minutes long, 'Ko Ko' ends abruptly, as if sheared off unresolved – which only adds to its punch. Swing music had reached a cul de sac: popular but artistically stuck. Charlie Parker had opened up a trailblazing new direction, and in doing so reinvented jazz.

'THE BEAT IN A BOP BAND IS WITH THE MUSIC, AGAINST IT, BEHIND IT. IT PUSHES IT. IT HELPS IT.'

CHARLIE PARKER

Jazz's freedom of expression, intellectual appreciation and eventual status as art music owes a sizeable debt to bebop.

Its prime movers – including alto saxophonist Charlie Parker and trumpeter Dizzy Gillespie – coupled formidable technical skills with deep knowledge of music theory. Serious-minded creators, they seemed cut from the same cloth as avant-garde composers such as Arnold Schoenberg or Igor Stravinsky (the latter a recognized influence on jazz). Starting in the early 1940s, from after-hours jams and play-offs at Harlem clubs such as Minton's (where Thelonious Monk was house pianist), they evolved a faster, less tuneful music with angular melodies, heavy on unpredictable rhythms, rapid chord changes and complex harmonies, whose bedrock was audacious improvisatory skills. It baffled swing fans while creating a hard core of aficionados – including Beat writers such as Jack Kerouac, whose prose crackled with bebop's propulsive rhythms and exhilarating outbursts.

Beboppers played in small combos, allowing each performer ample solo time, and fostered a new ethos: charting fresh musical territory was the goal, not audience pleasing; you didn't dance, you listened. Carefully. They operated outside showbusiness, unlike Louis Armstrong, Count Basie or Duke Ellington. Most were young African-Americans, and their exclusivity and musical brilliance also conveyed a thrilling sense of liberation, confidence and legitimacy – Black pride, in short.

Before the decade's end, younger practitioners such as Miles Davis were calming the tempos and note cascades and restoring arrangements and linear melodies – taking the heat out of bebop and birthing West Coast cool jazz. But by then it had already radically expanded the genre's palette, establishing myriad possibilities for modern jazz. Its after-tremors still resonate today – witness recordings by Robert Glasper and Kamasi Washington, both of whom mix traces of bebop with other styles to alchemize new forms.

THE SOUNDS OF SILENCE

4'33"
JOHN CAGE
1952

On 29 August 1952, David Tudor took to the stage at the Maverick Concert Hall in New York State, sat down at a piano and opened its lid. Over the next four and a half minutes, he closed and opened the lid several times (marking the end of one movement and the start of another). Then he rose and made his exit without having played a note. The audience were baffled, some enraged; very few understood that they'd just experienced a transformative moment in 20th-century music.

John Cage's *4'33"* is both childlike and profound. Those in the crowd that day who thought they'd heard nothing weren't listening. A wealth of ambient sounds filled that gap, from the noises of rainfall outside, to the scraping of chairs in the auditorium, and even the sound of one's own heartbeat. In conventional concerts, background noises are frowned upon; here, they were the 'composition' itself. A series of all-white paintings created the previous year by one of Cage's friends, the artist Robert Rauschenberg, was a key inspiration: a surface for light and shadow to play across, they weren't 'empty' at all.

As with Marcel Duchamp – one of his idols – there's a whiff of avant-garde prankster about Cage. But like Duchamp's readymades from the start of the century (found objects presented as art), *4'33"* was a solid conceptual leap into the dark that demands we re-evaluate what constitutes art. (Arnold Schoenberg, who taught Cage briefly, saw him as 'not a composer, but an inventor – of genius'.) Several of Cage's contemporary works, such as *Music of Changes* (1951), were influenced by his study of Zen Buddhism, which had led him to experiment with chance processes as a compositional tool to produce pieces as free as possible from ego and self. With *4'33"*, the content was entirely outside the composer's control. When listened to attentively, Cage suggests, all sound becomes music.

4' 33"

FOR ANY INSTRUMENT OR COMBINATION OF INSTRUMENTS

John Cage

One version of the sheet music for Cage's quiet revolution, from 1952 or 1953. In this transcription, he used vertical lines to represent the duration of the piece

THE BROAD CHURCH OF MINIMALISM

If Minimalism simply meant fewer musical components, then *4'33"* might be the definitive Minimalist statement. But the term is a richly amorphous one.

Another of its godfathers, Erik Satie, was dismissed by contemporary critics, but his rejection of Romanticism's grandiloquence (and the overarching influence of Richard Wagner) in favour of sparser and more repetitive textures proved pivotal. Satie's piano miniatures *Trois Gymnopédies* (1888) and *Trois Gnossiennes* (c.1890) spin beguiling variations around a core set of motifs. And in his theory of 'furniture music' – background balm to smooth out aural unpleasantness – he anticipated Brian Eno's experiments in ambient music during the 1970s.

A Minimalist work might incorporate space or silence, glacially shifting textures, rhythmic patterns criss-crossing like ripples, but also reassuring tonality. Terry Riley's pivotal composition *In C* (1964) acts as a slow reveal in which delicate fragmentary melodies play against a pulsing high C; refreshingly simple and unrestrictive, it represented a liberating release from the cul de sac of strictly composed, complex works by so many of Arnold Schoenberg's spiritual heirs (to whom repetition, open-endedness and tonality were no-go areas). Minimalism cut away that thorny musical brush and went back to the basics: pitch and rhythm. A shot of post-war American cheeriness to puncture the theory-bound European avant-garde.

Although John Cage was the first American musician to compose an entire piece with recording tape (1952's *Imaginary Landscape No.5*), Steve Reich broke new ground with *It's Gonna Rain* (1965), in which two loops of a street preacher's apocalyptic rant repeat on two tape machines that gradually slip out of sync ('phase shifting'). 'I want to be able to hear the process happening throughout the sounding music,' he explained in his 1968 essay 'Music as a Gradual Process'. Reich refined the concept in the Ghanaian-influenced *Drumming* (1971), in which performers' initially synced rhythms accumulate gloriously into a complex polyrhythmic tapestry.

Philip Glass at work in the early 2000s

Philip Glass came to a similar place via a different route: working with sitar master Ravi Shankar, it dawned on him that rhythms could become music's structural principle. But his 'classic' Minimalist works such as *Music in Twelve Parts* (1971–74) gave way to a more maximal approach with his revelatory (and very popular) five-hour opera *Einstein on the Beach* (1976), which reinvigorated the genre and launched Minimalism into the mainstream. Glass and Reich duly expanded their palettes to enable them to tackle themes with greater emotional, philosophical or political scope, such as Reich's Holocaust-referencing *Different Trains* (1988).

From the 1960s, Minimalist tropes also began infiltrating broader pop culture, injecting a then arresting unfamiliarity. Brian Eno worked with tape loops to create a string of mesmerizing ambient works in the 1970s, while Glass's soundtrack for *Koyaanisqatsi* (1982) evocatively complemented the theme of a world giddily out of balance.

THE RISE OF ROCK'N'ROLL

1954–1966

The post-war era was defined by clashing ideologies, the threat of conflict and racial unease. All of which was reflected in the music of the moment, which became more politicized.

After years of injustice, segregation was declared illegal by the US Supreme Court in 1954 – the year Elvis Presley made his first recordings – but it remained a fact of life in Southern states, and musicians would become part of complex cultural debates. Elvis Presley and his rock'n'roll brethren were pilloried by some for embracing 'coloured' musical styles; others would claim he had a role in uniting whites and Blacks. ('The white kids had to hide my records 'cos they daren't let their parents know they had them in the house,' recalled Little Richard.) Elsewhere, two white Jewish songwriters, Jerry Leiber and Mike Stoller, penned imperishable tracks for Black performers such as Big Mama Thornton and the Coasters (and eventually Elvis himself).

In 1955, after Rosa Parks refused to give up her seat to a white man in Montgomery, Alabama, there was a city-wide bus boycott. By the early 1960s, such 'Freedom Rides' were a common strategy for the burgeoning civil rights movement, which had the inspirational Reverend Martin Luther King Jr as one of its leading lights. In the early 1970s, Motown's Berry Gordy Jr would release speeches by King, and spoken-word pieces by activist Stokely Carmichael and poets Langston Hughes and Margaret Danner on his Black Forum label.

In tandem, a revival of folk music in America that had begun in the 1940s acquired new urgency and impetus with the rise of singer-songwriters including Bob Dylan, Joan Baez and Phil Ochs. Touted (though it irked him) as the voice of his generation, Dylan offered caustic commentary on discrimination, nuclear armageddon and sabre-rattling with instant anthems such as 'Oxford Town', 'Talking World War III Blues' and 'Masters of War'.

In late 1956, a fledgling revolution in Hungary against the Soviet-backed Hungarian People's Republic was brutally quashed. The following year, Russia's *Sputnik* satellite launched, inaugurating a 'Space Race' with the USA. Initially, the Soviets seemed to be on top: in 1961, Yuri Gagarin became the first man in space. But 1962 saw the launch of NASA's *Telstar 1*, the world's first active communications satellite. Wildcard British producer Joe Meek celebrated the event with the Tornados' 'Telstar', featuring the sci-fi wail of an electronic keyboard, which became the first US No.1 by a British group.

By 1960, the US government was presided over by the youthful President John F. Kennedy. The Soviets erected a wall dividing East from West Berlin in 1961 and Cuba continued to be a thorn in Kennedy's side. The arrival of Soviet missiles on the island prompted a tense 13-day political stand-off between the USA and the Soviet Union in 1962.

With Elvis a GI in Germany, a wave of bequiffed male wannabes with none of his provocative aura emerged. More interestingly, into the vacuum also stepped girl groups, often women of colour (the Shirelles, the Crystals, the Ronettes). Much of their era-defining work was penned by brilliant songwriting partnerships collectively associated with New York's Brill Building. Producer Phil Spector turned many of their songs into towering pop statements with his immense 'Wall of Sound' arrangements.

For all his conservatism, President Kennedy seemed to personify a new optimism in the USA – economic growth doubled under him – making his assassination on 22 November 1963 all the more shocking. Plenty of US teenagers found relief in the arrival of the Beatles there in February 1964, heralding a new 'British Invasion' of music Stateside. They would be photographed with Cassius Clay – shortly to become world heavyweight boxing champion – though he'd change his name to Muhammad Ali after aligning himself with the Nation of Islam and its charismatic, provocative leader, Malcolm X. By 1966, there were already mass protests against the Vietnam War. Ali refused to fight and was stripped of his world title.

Pop music wore a Janus face that year, torn between the familiar and the avant-garde: Tom Jones's 'Green, Green Grass of Home' and the Beatles' 'Tomorrow Never Knows'. Jones's tune, a wistful country song, nodded to the past. The Beatles' track was a taster for pop's Next Big Thing: psychedelia.

'IT APPEALS TO THE BASE IN MAN, BRINGS OUT ANIMALISM AND VULGARITY.'

ASA E. CARTER, NORTH ALABAMA CITIZENS COUNCIL, ON ROCK'N'ROLL

1954

→ Algerian resistance against French colonialism begins; the country will finally become liberated in 1962.

→ Pierre Boulez composes his avant-garde masterpiece *Le Marteau sans maître*.

→ Appearance of the first commercial transistor radio, IDEA's Regency TR-1.

→ Premiere of *On the Waterfront*, directed by Elia Kazan.

→ 'Rock Around the Clock' by Bill Haley and His Comets is released. It becomes the inaugural rock'n'roll hit to make No.1 in the USA (and UK, where it becomes the country's first million-seller).

1955

→ 'Maybellene' gives rock'n'roll pioneer Chuck Berry his debut US Top 5 hit.

→ Release of Little Richard's 'Tutti Frutti'.

→ Publication of Vladimir Nabokov's novel *Lolita*.

→ Lonnie Donegan's 'Rock Island Line' helps kickstart the UK's skiffle craze.

→ The McDonald's fast-food chain launches.

1956

→ Egypt's nationalization of the Suez Canal under President Gamal Abdel Nasser prompts political panic and an invasion by British, French and Israeli forces.

→ An uprising in Hungary against Soviet rule is swiftly crushed.

1957

→ Launch of the first satellite, the Soviet *Sputnik*.

1958

→ Elvis Presley enlists in the US Army.

→ NASA is created.

1959

→ Buddy Holly, Ritchie Valens and the 'Big Bopper' (J. P. Richardson) perish in a plane crash – 'The Day the Music Died'.

1960

→ Police in Sharpeville, South Africa, confront 7,000 protesters, killing 69 of them, with 180 more injured.

→ Federico Fellini's *La Dolce Vita* premieres.

1961
→ Yuri Gagarin becomes the first astronaut in space.
→ Patent for the earliest integrated circuit is issued in the USA.
→ Peter Benenson founds Amnesty International.

1962
→ The placement of Soviet weapons on Cuba results in a tense two-week stand-off between President Khrushchev of the USSR and the USA's President Kennedy: the Cuban Missile Crisis.
→ Soul star Ray Charles releases the genre-blending milestone *Modern Sounds in Country and Western Music*.
→ Pop artist Andy Warhol's *Campbell's Soup Cans* screen prints go on display.

1963
→ The Ronettes' 'Be My Baby' and the Crystals' 'Da Doo Ron Ron', both released this year, encapsulate Phil Spector's era-defining Wall of Sound productions.

1964
→ For one week in April, the Beatles hold the top five places on the *Billboard* Hot 100.
→ Robert Moog completes the first Moog syntheziser.
→ Japan's Shinkansen bullet train is launched.
→ Marshall McLuhan proposes the concept of a 'global village' and coins the phrase 'the medium is the message'.
→ Sidney Poitier becomes the first Black recipient of the Best Actor Oscar for his appearance in *Lilies of the Field* (1963).

1965
→ The initial influx of US troops arrives in Vietnam.
→ Mary Quant launches the mini skirt.
→ The Rolling Stones' signature song '(I Can't Get No) Satisfaction' becomes a global chart-topper.
→ Bob Dylan's six-minute-plus 'Like a Rolling Stone' becomes a global smash, shattering conventions about how long a single should be.
→ Release of John Coltrane's *A Love Supreme* album.

1966
→ The Black Panther Party forms in Oakland, California.
→ The Beach Boys' *Pet Sounds* is released.

THE HILLBILLY CAT TAKES OFF

'THAT'S ALL RIGHT' / 'BLUE MOON OF KENTUCKY'
ELVIS PRESLEY
1954

It's hard now to appreciate the stir Elvis's first single caused. 'That's All Right Mama' was originally a single by bluesman Arthur 'Big Boy' Crudup in 1946. 'Blue Moon of Kentucky' was a sedate bluegrass waltz from a couple of years later by Bill Monroe. What Elvis did (along with guitarist Scotty Moore and stand-up bassist Bill Black) was add a country lilt to the former – check out Moore's Chet Atkins-inflected guitar picking – and an R&B swing to the latter, which they also sped up and changed to 4/4 time. That caused confusion aplenty: was the singer Black or white? What kind of music was this, anyway?

At its heart, Elvis's wondrous vocal was confident, vibrant, popping with life – like a Louis Armstrong Hot Five solo – and couched in the slap-back echo that made the sound of Sam Phillips's Sun records so thrilling.

Reaction was immediate and overwhelming. The first night Memphis DJ Dewey Phillips spun an acetate of 'That's All Right', he was swamped with calls and gave it repeat plays. But this odd hybrid music raised hackles too (although Bill Haley and His Comets had done something similar with 1952's 'Rock the Joint'). Shreveport country DJ T. Tommy Cutrer told Phillips that if he played it he'd be run out of town. R&B DJ Fats Washington did play it, but announced on air: 'This man should not be played after the sun comes up in the morning, it's so country.' When Elvis performed it live – all greased-back DA haircut, gyrating legs and out-there threads from Memphis's Beale Street (he favoured black and pink) – the buzz skyrocketed. 'There was just no reference point in the culture to compare it,' marvelled Roy Orbison, who saw the trio in Texas as a 19-year-old.

All that fuss would have felt impossible in early June 1954, when Elvis, Scotty and Bill made 'That's All Right'. The session dragged, inspiration nowhere to be found. They took a break. And then, as a joke, Elvis started goofing around on Crudup's song; Scotty and Bill fell right in. Sam Phillips stuck his head out of the control booth, asked them what they were doing, told them to begin again and began recording. It was the same when they came to record the flip side: nothing stuck until Bill started fooling around on 'Blue Moon of Kentucky'. 'Hell, that's different,' Phillips told the trio. 'That's a pop song now, nearly about.'

Elvis taped some 24 tracks with Phillips, before the latter sold him to RCA Victor in late 1955. Phillips selected the upbeat ones for Presley's five singles on Sun – though Elvis's inclination was for slow, faintly melancholy ballads (as with his first RCA single, 'Heartbreak Hotel'). Like 'That's All Right', they're drumless, and they frequently swing rather than attack, an energizing and sassy blend of white (country, bluegrass) and Black (blues, R&B) music. In a word: rockabilly.

Elvis and his band debut 'Heartbreak Hotel' on the Dorsey Brothers' *Stage Show*, 1956

Rock'n'roll's origins are murky and non-linear. Phillips also recorded Ike Turner and his band at Sun, and their 'Rocket 88' (credited to Jackie Brenston and his Delta Cats), released in 1951, is often cited as the first rock'n'roll single. Then again, so is Arthur Crudup's original take on 'That's All Right'. Listen to gospel performer Sister Rosetta Tharpe's holler and guitar solos on 1938's 'That's All' and 'Rock Me' with her boogie-woogie pianist Albert Ammons, or 1944's 'Strange Things Happening Every Day': isn't that the essence of rock'n'roll? 'Rock'n'roll was here a long time before I came along,' Elvis stated flatly. 'Let's face it: I can't sing like Fats Domino can. I know that.'

RCA's attempt to mimic Sun's slap-back echo on 'Heartbreak Hotel' didn't come off, but the brooding track gave Elvis his first *Billboard* No.1. Cue stellar success... and uproar, his performances censored on TV and press coverage that not infrequently compared him to a stripper.

But the cameras loved him. And he was white; it's worth remembering that given the racial iniquities of the era, sponsors avoided patronizing TV shows with mixed-race performers, for fear of ostracizing certain areas of the country. No Black artist, however talented, could have achieved Elvis's rise back then: 'We had people who could do it better than him but who couldn't be accepted at that time because of the colour of their skin,' jazz trumpeter Wynton Marsalis once stated. But that's not to say that his success wasn't helpful. 'I thank the Lord for sending Elvis to open that door,' Little Richard declared in 1970, 'so I could walk down the road, you understand?'

'I ALWAYS KNEW THAT THE REBELLION OF YOUNG PEOPLE, WHICH IS AS NATURAL AS BREATHING, WOULD BE A PART OF THAT BREAKTHROUGH.'

SAM PHILLIPS

Little Richard steals the show in 1956 rock flick *The Girl Can't Help It*

Rock'n'roll's first global chart-topper was 'Rock Around the Clock' by Bill Haley and His Comets in 1954, whose homely leader was 30 at the time. Chuck Berry was just a year younger, but if rock'n'roll has an architect, it's him. Berry penned witty songs that encapsulated teenage life (perhaps his closest peer as a singer/songwriter was Buddy Holly). His vibrant guitar-playing and showmanship both established genre templates.

No one sang like Little Richard, though. His high-voltage 'Tutti Frutti' (way too lascivious for radioplay with its original lyrics) opened with rock'n'roll's most famous yowl.

Elvis's Sun labelmate, Jerry Lee Lewis, matched keyboard fireworks with swaggering vocals. Another prime mover, Fats Domino, enjoyed huge sales purveying a warmer and less frenzied update of R&B and boogie-woogie. Gene Vincent, however, shared some of Lewis's unhinged edginess, audibly so on his twitchy signature hit 'Be-Bop-A-Lula'.

The army (Elvis), church (Little Richard), prison (Chuck Berry) and scandal (Jerry Lee Lewis) took out four of them; others lost their mojo or died too young. But by then they'd charted a course for what was to happen in the next decade.

'I SING THE BODY ELECTRIC'

GESANG DER JÜNGLINGE
KARLHEINZ STOCKHAUSEN
1955–56

A turning point in electronic composition, *Gesang der Jünglinge* set Stockhausen apart even from fellow travellers such as the Pierres Schaeffer and Henry, who were then still working exclusively with found sounds.

Stockhausen had the idea of writing a mixed vocal/electronic mass for Cologne Cathedral (at the time, he was a still a Catholic). The authorities considered loudspeakers unacceptable in this sacred space, but he adapted that original concept to create a shorter work utilizing 'Song of the Youths', an apocryphal text from the Book of Daniel in which God saves three innocents from a furnace after they are thrown there for refusing to worship an idol.

Stockhausen had studied phonetics, and his complex working methods for *Gesang der Jünglinge* involved dissecting the original passage into the smallest possible units of human speech (from phrases to syllables and even phonemes). He devised a system of electronically generated tones and timbres, each of which mirrored a facet of the sung text – pure sine-wave tones for vowels, clicks for plosives (for example, the sound of 'b', 'd' or 'k'), and filtered white noise for consonants. His graphic notations of the melodies were then sung multiple times – to ensure vocal purity, the performer was a 12-year-old chorister, Josef Protschka – and layered. The two elements were then laboriously woven together to produce an unprecedented work comprising acoustic voice, electronically generated sounds and a blend of both.

With further recording and treatment, it took well over a year, even with the participation of assistants, for the painstaking process to result in a composition 13 minutes 14 seconds long, divided into six sections. The rich sonic palette takes in brief vocal snippets and a choral flourish rising from nowhere and swiftly disappearing, sci-fi-style burbles and surges or bird-like twitters. But whenever there is a clearly audible line, it offers praise to God.

Gesang's premiere at Cologne's Westdeutscher Rundfunk studio on 30 May 1956 was characteristically innovative. Stockhausen placed four sets of loudspeakers around the audience, with a fifth above, surrounding them in a five-pointed sonic net, within which the sound swirled and switched direction.

Following this breakthrough, Stockhausen became perhaps the pre-eminent post-war avant-gardist. But if *Gesang der Jünglinge* was a song of praise, it also reflected his struggles with forging this new music and the criticism his early works had attracted. 'From 1954 to 1956 was a unique time of jubilantly praising God,' he remembered. 'And I myself was "a youth in the fiery furnace".'

Stockhausen, who match-maked *elektronische Musik* with *musique concrète*

THE RISE OF ROCK'N'ROLL 1954–1966

THE VANGUARD OF ELECTRONIC MUSIC

In 1944, Egyptian innovator Halim El-Dabh created probably the earliest electronic composition, the haunting 25-minute *Ta'abir Al-Zaar*. Having used a wire recorder to record a *zaar* – a healing ceremony sung by women – he treated it with echo and reverb, removed selected frequencies, and then transferred it to reel-to-reel tape for further manipulation. In performance, sound is fleeting; El-Dabh had captured it and altered it.

In Paris, radio engineer Pierre Schaeffer was working in a similar vein, and in 1948, he created *Cinq études de bruits*. Although looped and edited, his source recordings are clearly recognizable – as an original composition, El-Dabh's creation is more successful. But as with artist Marcel Duchamp and his 'readymades', Schaeffer was divorcing sounds from their original context and re-presenting them as art – sampling, in all but name. He dubbed it *musique concrète*: found sounds, as opposed to found objects.

Along with composer Pierre Henry and engineer Jacques Poullin, Schaeffer went on to establish the experimental Groupe de Récherches Musciales (GRM) studio in 1951, based in the city's Radiodiffusion-Télévision Française. Why a state broadcaster? In the pre-synthesizer world, only organizations with generous budgets – and plenty of space – could afford bulky cutting-edge electronic equipment.

A hothouse of electro-acoustic investigations, the GRM attracted the likes of Karlheinz Stockhausen (who worked on sound analysis there for a while), Edgard Varèse and Iannis Xenakis. In Cologne, an electronic studio at Westdeutscher Runkfunk (WDR) studio, where Stockhausen became an assistant in 1953, focused on pure *elektronische Musik* rather than transforming found acoustic sounds.

Bebe Barron and her husband Louis composed the first fully electronic movie soundtrack for sci-fi film *Forbidden Planet* (1956), created by building electronic circuits to generate sounds. The couple processed the resulting tapes, then edited and multitracked them. To anticipate interference from the Musician's Union, studio MGM foreswore any

Delia Derbyshire at the BBC Radiophonic Workshop

reference to this as 'music', crediting the Barrons instead with creating 'electronic tonalities'.

Co-founder of the BBC Radiophonic Workshop (which devised unusual sonorities for drama productions), Daphne Oram had utilized a tape recorder, sine-wave oscillator and self-made filters to create a soundtrack for a TV adaptation of the play *Amphitryon 38*; shown in March 1958, it represented the first airing of an electronic score on UK television sets. One of the Workshop's outstanding talents, Delia Derbyshire, brought experimental electronic music into UK households every week: composed in 1963, her startling arrangement of Ron Grainer's theme tune to *Doctor Who* incorporated sizzling white noise and the surging sounds of test oscillators. Distressingly, Derbyshire was denied even co-authorship, despite Rainer's exasperated pleas; to the staid BBC, she was an assistant studio manager and as such was doomed to remain anonymous.

ON THE MODE

KIND OF BLUE
MILES DAVIS
1959

Bebop rattled and reconfigured jazz in the 1940s. Davis had been part of that episode, but with *Kind of Blue* he engineered a very different kind of radical shift, something more like a velvet revolution.

At its core, Davis's quest to simplify: 'The music has gotten thick,' he complained to Nat Hentoff of *The Jazz Review* the previous year, citing the complicated chord arrangements that had become common in modern jazz, and arguing for 'a return to emphasis on melodic rather than harmonic variation. There will be fewer chords but infinite possibilities as to what to do with them.' Davis's solution – one that he'd already explored on the title track of the hard bop *Milestones* (1958) – was to go modal: to improvise on a scale ('mode'), or several, rather than over a complex set of chords.

He wanted it to sound fresh too, and to that end came up with the settings for each piece scant hours before the recordings, arriving at the studio with sketches for the group he'd assembled. They were given hardly any rehearsal time either, an approach that had become synonymous with Davis, for whom, as for Bob Dylan, imperfections added spice to the sound. 'Therefore,' noted pianist Bill Evans in the album's liner notes, 'you will hear something close to pure spontaneity in these performances.' Evans had actually left Davis's band by this point, but was recalled for the recording as Davis had structured the album around his playing.

It was recorded over the course of two sessions at Columbia's 30th Street Studio, New York, in March and April 1959. To realize Davis's demands required sidemen of the highest calibre, as they'd be asked to create melodic improvisation with only the barest preparation. The group is acknowledged as one of the greatest jazz ensembles ever put together: alongside Evans, Davis recruited John Coltrane on tenor sax, Wynton Kelly (on piano for one track only), 'Cannonball' Adderley on alto sax, Paul Chambers on bass and Jimmy Cobb on drums.

Even on the more upbeat numbers (the nine-minute opener 'So What', for example – which became one of Davis's signature pieces – and 'All Blues') there's an unrushed quality to the playing, space built in to the sound. Mostly, though, the tempo is slow, with measured solos flowing back and forth in a perfectly balanced democracy and no performer dominant. On the gentler numbers, such as the closing 'Flamenco Sketches', the music seems dreamily open, with the potential to drift on forever.

It took a while for *Kind of Blue*'s understated majesty to find its audience. For one thing, at around the same period alto saxophonist Ornette Coleman was

Genius of a different stripe. A dapper Miles around the time of the release of *Kind of Blue*

THE RISE OF ROCK'N'ROLL 1954–1966

making waves with his own ground-breaking sound, which would come to be known as 'free jazz' (see opposite), as heard on his much-lauded *The Shape of Jazz to Come* – recorded the month after *Kind of Blue* and released three months later. That irked Davis, who didn't find the new innovations all that revolutionary, although he acknowledged, 'He just came and fucked up everybody.'

Down the decades, *Kind of Blue*'s appeal has touched countless musicians, many working outside the jazz idiom. In his liner notes for the 1997 re-release of the album, Robert Palmer recalled guitarist Duane Allman telling him, 'I've listened to that album so many times that for the past couple of years, I haven't hardly listened to anything else.'

You don't need to know that these songs are based on a modal template to appreciate them. Innovative but accessible, their lyricism appeals to musicians and non-musicians alike – one of the reasons that the album, as well as being one of the most influential in the history of jazz, is also a five-times platinum bestseller. And, even more remarkably, retains its zest to this day.

'THERE WILL BE FEWER CHORDS BUT INFINITE POSSIBILITIES AS TO WHAT TO DO WITH THEM.'

MILES DAVIS

'I thought [the saxophone] was a toy and I just played it. Didn't know you have to learn something to find out what the toy does.' Ornette Coleman

Part of the 'freedom' in free jazz (the term comes from a 1960 Coleman album) involved dispensing with conventions such as regular meter or harmonic progression. Accents fell in odd places and melodies had uneven lengths; tempos quickened and slowed within a piece. Compositions bustled with atonal awkwardness and polyrhythms – to some, simply anarchy; to others, unfettered liberation. 'I play pure emotion,' Coleman insisted.

His quartet comprised only solo instruments (Don Cherry on horn, with Charlie Haden and Billy Higgins on bass and drums), nothing that could play harmonies, such as a piano. This tied in with Coleman's concept of 'Harmolodics': improvisation based on melody, not harmony or chord changes. John Coltrane was to incorporate free jazz techniques such as overblowing to expand the palette of his tenor saxophone. Charles Mingus admired the freshness of Coleman's 'notes and lines', while the liberating openness of free jazz informed the trajectory maverick spirits such as Sun Ra and Pharaoh Sanders.

MUSIC TO SCREAM TO

'SHE LOVES YOU'
THE BEATLES
1963

That year, they'd already scored their first UK No.1 ('From Me To You'), while their done-in-a-day debut LP would top the charts for 30 weeks. Audience hysteria was escalating at gigs. But their fourth single, 'She Loves You', blew the roof off pop.

The opening drum roll, like an avalanche; the fizzing hi-hat splashes throughout. The punchy vocals, rising to falsetto before the chorus explodes, and ending the song on a triumphant major sixth – a harmony that their producer, George Martin, advised them was hackneyed: it smacked of Glenn Miller and his wartime dance-band arrangements. They didn't care; it sounded good.

With some half a million in pre-orders, 'She Loves You' hit No.1 for a month, dropped off and then (rarely for the time) regained the top spot. The single's impact resonated far beyond the pages of *NME* and *Melody Maker*, however. 'She Loves You' made the Beatles national news – definitively so when it closed their set on TV's *Sunday Night at the London Palladium* that October. Liverpool FC's Kop sang it at Anfield. The refrain's 'yeah, yeah, yeahs' became an instant trademark, and the 'ooo' falsettos invariably raised fans' frenzy in concert when accompanied by mop-top-tossing head-shakes from Paul McCartney and George Harrison.

A joyous burst of power pop, 'She Loves You' summed up Beatlemania in two minutes 18 seconds. It also signposted greater things to come. On 10 December, CBS anchorman Walter Cronkite ended his broadcast with a short clip of the group, featuring 'She Loves You', for some light relief – President John F. Kennedy's assassination had dominated coverage for weeks. Fifteen-year-old Marsha Albert saw it and wrote to DJ Carroll James of Washington station WWDC, asking him to play more by the group. James brought her in to introduce their new UK single, 'I Want to Hold Your Hand', which got an ecstatic reaction from listeners. He sent the tape to DJs in Chicago and St Louis: same story. Alerted to the wildfire of enthusiasm, Capitol released the song on 26 December; marketing did the rest and within four weeks it was America's No.1. 'She Loves You' followed suit. On the *Billboard* Hot 100 of 4 April 1964, the group had all five top positions. Blink and you'd miss the milestones as they flew by.

After years of subservience to American artists and musical trends, British pop was suddenly hot in the USA.

That can't be bad: the Fabs in the first flush of Beatlemania

THE RISE OF ROCK'N'ROLL 1954–1966

THE BRITISH INVASION

Around 40 per cent of the American population tuned in to watch the Beatles' US debut on *The Ed Sullivan Show* on 9 February 1964. In the two years or so after that unprecedented breakthrough, British groups found the USA newly welcoming – part of a contemporary Anglophile cross-cultural shift that was also felt in movies and fashion. In 1965, half the *Billboard* No.1s were by British artists.

Some were pure pop and enjoyed huge hits. Others changed the identity of American popular music more fundamentally, partly by revisiting its own overlooked or forgotten riches – not least original material by Black artists that had been covered, cleaned up or appropriated to become hits for white performers. In their cover versions and interviews, the Beatles championed US girl groups, first-generation rock'n'rollers such as Chuck Berry, and Motown.

Bob Dylan had covered the standard 'House of the Rising Sun' on his 1962 debut LP, but its electrified reinterpretation by the Animals – a transatlantic No.1 in 1964 – transfixed him. The following year's half-electric, half-acoustic *Bringing It All Back Home* suggested it had left its mark.

The Rolling Stones were devotees of hardcore blues and R&B (ditto the Animals and Pretty Things). These were still cult markets in the UK during the early 1960s, with a non-conformist cachet. The Stones' edgier, more sexually overt material made them the rebel teenager's group of choice. They became a major influence on the garage bands of mid-60s America – the Chocolate Watchband, the Standells, the Seeds and their ilk.

Like the Animals, the Kinks made an immediate and profound impact. Their 'You Really Got Me' and 'All Day and All of the Night' (two US Top 10s) reworked the primal bawl of the Kingsmen's 'Louie Louie' with a dirty guitar tone, and the group were regulars on US TV pop shows. Both songs became garage-rock staples, alongside the likes of 'Gloria' (by Van Morrison's Them) and the Troggs' 'Wild Thing'.

With Eric Clapton as lead guitarist, The Yardbirds developed their own mid-song 'rave up' sections,

Pop-art punks. The Who stare down the camera, 1965

ratcheting up the tempo, volume and momentum –
a trick adopted by numerous contemporary US bands.
(Think of the Count Five's uptight 'Psychotic
Reaction', a US No.5.) With Clapton replaced by Jeff
Beck and later Jimmy Page, such passages evolved
naturally into psychedelically tinged improvisation
live, while the increasingly hard-edged sound of the
band's final incarnation under Page informed his next
band, Led Zeppelin.

Heavily identified with the very British mod
phenomenon, the Who took longer to catch on than
most. When they finally broke the USA with *Tommy*
(1969), the 'invasion' had run its course. But by then it
had reinvigorated the American music scene at a time
when home-grown rock'n'roll had lost its pep.

THE DUAL LIFE OF A SONG

'DANCING IN THE STREET'
MARTHA AND THE VANDELLAS
1964

To Martha Reeves, it was a party song.

She'd cut the vocal in Motown's Studio A in June 1964. After a fine first take, one of the song's co-authors, Ivy Jo Hunter, told her they hadn't been recording. She'd have to sing it again. That irritated Reeves, and her second run-through, joyous though it was, had a bite that the first take lacked. Hunter had suspected as much, which was why he'd come up with the ruse in the first place.

Martha and the Vandellas' two previous singles had stiffed, but 'Dancing in the Street' packed an open-hearted euphoria that was impossible to ignore, or sit still to, out-punching anything the Supremes had done. Superficially, it was simply a neat hook to include a roll call of US cities to join in the dance – a trick Chuck Berry ('Sweet Little Sixteen'), among others, had already employed – though tellingly, all were places with significant Black populations (the idea came from the co-writer of 'Dancing in the Street', Marvin Gaye). 'Dancing in the Street' took the group to No.2 on *Billboard*'s Hot 100 – their highest-ever showing.

But among the clarion-call horns and crashing backbeats there was something else. Gaye heard it, and in the Vandellas' urgent 'Nowhere to Run' and 'Wild One' too. 'Of all the acts back then, I thought Martha and the Vandellas came closest to really saying something,' he told biographer David Ritz. 'It wasn't a conscious thing, but . . . they captured a spirit that felt political to me.' He wasn't alone.

Urban conflict was ripping across America. The 1964 Civil Rights Act formalized desegregation in public places in the USA and, nominally at least, outlawed discrimination against Black citizens. But that year's 'Freedom Summer' – a voter registration drive to boost levels of Black voters in Mississippi – prompted arrests, beatings and murders: Black churches firebombed; police brutality rife; a Ku Klux Klan revival; riots in Harlem, in Watts, in Newark; confidence waning in the government, but in non-violent protest too. And in that febrile atmosphere, 'Dancing in the Street' took on new meaning.

It fitted the times. Its galvanizing energy found a radical new context – disillusioned protesters – and plenty in the counterculture read it as a vibrant call to arms. Activist H. Rap Brown played the song at rallies. Left-wing militants the Weathermen assumed that the tune was a musical incitement to take the battle to the streets of America and the world beyond. Reeves was singing it onstage at Detroit's Fox Theatre one July night in 1967 when she got the message to stop. Prompted by a police raid, a crowd of angry protesters had cut loose in the city, looting and torching – violence on a scale unseen in America since a Civil War-era draft riot. She was advised to tell the audience to go home.

Detroit chic: Martha and her Vandellas

THE RISE OF ROCK'N'ROLL 1954–1966

That same year, Aretha Franklin had a hit with her cover of Otis Redding's 'Respect'. Franklin triumphantly reworked the song as a demand for equality on all levels – whether that be physical attention from a man to his woman, or a dignified equality between the races. For all the militant connotations heaped on it in the tumultuous late 1960s, 'Dancing in the Street''s enduring message seems a spiritual sibling to Franklin's. Mickey Stevenson – Motown's A&R man, Martha Reeves' mentor and the song's third co-author – was driving around Detroit in the summer of 1964 with Marvin Gaye. Children of all races were playing in the water gushing from fire hydrants – effortless integration.

Reeves always maintained that nothing political had been hotwired into the song at its creation. But one experience from the singer's teenage years in Detroit did give it a personal resonance for her as a song of liberation from oppression. Gatherings of Black civilians in public places weren't tolerated and an armed police unit, known as the 'Big Four', regularly prevented Reeves and her friends from congregating for doo-wop sessions on street corners, harassing or arresting them. For Martha Reeves, it was a song about feeling utterly free. Or as she put it, decades later: 'You don't have to worry about cars hitting you. You don't have to worry about policemen coming and telling you you can't dance in the street.'

'THE MOTOWN SOUND WAS A VERY BIG INFLUENCE IN THE CIVIL RIGHTS MOVEMENT. IT WAS NOT THAT WE MARCHED OR PARADED; WE JUST PROMOTED IT THROUGH LOVE.'

MARTHA REEVES

A Black record company, with a multiracial staff, that could thrive in the white-controlled industry? As the Four Tops' Duke Fakir put it, Motown made white America 'begin to look at Black America a little differently. It's one of the steps that took us up that ladder.'

Stung by industry practices as a songwriter, Berry Gordy Jr founded his own label, Tamla, in January 1959, building an astonishing roster of artists, including Marvin Gaye, the Supremes, the Four Tops, Martha and the Vandellas, and the Temptations. In Gaye, Smokey Robinson and Holland-Dozier-Holland, he had some of the era's finest songwriters too, and a top-notch studio band in the Funk Brothers.

Gordy had worked at a Ford plant in Detroit, and brought an assembly-line mentality to his family of labels, most famously Motown (a nod to Detroit's nickname 'Motor City'). Performers learned deportment alongside dance steps and were impeccably dressed. Releases were stringently vetted; trends were studied. The music was melodic, pop-friendly R&B and soul appealing to teenagers across racial lines – 'the Sound of Young America', in an inspired slogan.

From 1960 to 1969, Motown and its associated labels scored 79 hits on the *Billboard* Hot 100, first topping the listings in 1961 with the Marvelettes' 'Please Mr. Postman' and including five straight No.1s with the Supremes. Gordy wanted uncontroversial songs, and for his artists to play prestigious clubs such as the Copacabana, performing standards alongside the pop to expand and extend their careers.

By the later 1960s, Motown seemed out of step, especially against the grittier soul of Memphis's Stax. In 1967, the label had a front-row seat at Detroit's devastating riots, prompted by endemic racial discrimination. Somewhat grudgingly, it embraced more socially engaged material – and gained a new lease of life.

FUNK HITS THE *BILLBOARD* TOP 10

'PAPA'S GOT A BRAND NEW BAG'
JAMES BROWN
1965

By 1965, R&B and soul shouter *in excelsis* James Brown was sketching out a compelling new music in concert, one based less on melody than rhythm. The road to funk.

He'd had the germ of the idea for a while, getting close on the 1962 B-side 'I've Got Money', though there the drums provide a skittering fill throughout and the brass is full. Brown himself saw 1964's more stripped-down 'Out of Sight' as the first funk record, though despite the staccato rhythms and clipped brass interjections, it swings a little too much.

'Papa's Got a Brand New Bag' reworks that track as something leaner and harder. Its very title acknowledges the change. The arrangement is less cluttered, with more space; the guitar and brass make sharp interjections. Unlike contemporary releases from soul-oriented labels such as Stax or Motown, the song stutters, with a stop-start movement, the emphasis firmly 'on the one' (the first beat of a four-beat bar) as opposed to the backbeat (the two and four). Live, the instrumental-only passages allowed Brown to focus on his showmanship.

Released as a two-part single, it gave him his first *Billboard* Top 10 hit (and spent eight weeks atop the R&B listings). As funk's first major hit, its success helped to broadcast Brown's new direction – which was cemented with the follow-up, 'I Got You (I Feel Good)', an even bigger hit. Future releases would further strip down the chord changes and vocals, placing even greater emphasis on the rhythm as the engine to propel a song forward. 'I had discovered that my strength was not in the horns, it was in the rhythm,' Brown explained later. 'I was hearing everything, even the guitar, like they were drums.' In doing so, in retrospect, it implicitly connected the roots of R&B (and soul, and the blues, and by extension rock'n'roll) with African percussive traditions, something that would chime with the rise of Black empowerment and Afrocentrism in due course.

He'd seal the deal two years later with 'Cold Sweat', complete with drum solo/breakbeat, a feature that became a funk staple and a rich source of samples for hip-hop artists. By 1970's 'Get Up (I Feel Like Being a) Sex Machine', Brown's innovations were audible in the work of everyone from Sly and the Family Stone to Miles Davis. But his vision of funk first caught the world's ears with 'Papa's Got a Brand New Bag'.

The Hardest-Working Man in Show Business, dressed up to drop the funk

THE RISE OF ROCK'N'ROLL 1954–1966

'THE OLD ORDER CHANGETH, YIELDING PLACE TO NEW'

BOB DYLAN 'GOES ELECTRIC'
AT THE NEWPORT FOLK FESTIVAL
1965

'I don't want to write for people anymore,' Bob Dylan told *Life* magazine in 1964. 'I want to write from inside me.' That year, the 'British Invasion' swept into America, with the Beatles in the vanguard, inspiring a triumphant resurgence of rock'n'roll. And in his high-school yearbook, Dylan had stated his ambition as 'to join Little Richard'.

In March 1965, he released *Bringing it all Back Home*, the first side of which was all-electric, the title a reminder to Brits of where it all began. It kicked off with 'Subterranean Homesick Blues', a scattershot panorama of the changing times that rattled some aficionados of his earlier 'protest' songs.

Newport was at the epicentre of America's folk revival. To traditionalists at the festival, rock'n'roll was capitalism and commercialism personified, nothing to do with contemporary political imperatives. The old guard dressed in workshirts and denim, not Carnaby Street frippery.

On the afternoon of 25 July, sporting sunglasses, a polka-dot shirt and Beatles-style ankle boots, Dylan jammed at Newport Folk Festival with a scratch band that included Al Kooper on organ and Mike Bloomfield on guitar. That night, he took to the stage wearing a leather jacket and Fender Stratocaster. The group tore into a ragged 'Maggie's Farm' and the boos started, mixed with shrieks of delight; derision from many, but amazement from others at the energy coming off the stage, Bloomfield's solos shrieking through the night. They did two more songs, including 'Like a Rolling Stone' (released four days earlier, it had been blasting out of transistor radios all weekend), then walked off.

Perhaps Dylan was dazed by the reception and had tears in his eyes; folk icon Pete Seeger certainly did. Perhaps the catcalls were because the instruments drowned out his vocals, or the PA system couldn't handle a volume that, for the time, was extreme. There'd been little time to balance the sound and the band were certainly under-rehearsed.

He was encouraged to come back (Dylan was headlining, so some in the crowd doubtless felt short-changed too), performed two more songs solo with an acoustic guitar ('It's All Over Now, Baby Blue' – the writing on the wall right there – and 'Mr Tambourine Man'), and left again, this time to a standing ovation.

Dylan's subsequent world tour was Newport many times over, his band buffeted by jeers and heckles (including, infamously, 'Judas!' at Manchester Free Trade Hall in 1966). But he was an artist. And artists don't look back.

An electric atmosphere: Dylan at Newport

REVOLUTION FROM STUDIO TO STREET

1967–1976

It was first synthesized in 1938, but lysergic acid diethylamide (LSD) only became the counterculture's drug of choice from the mid-60s onwards. On America's West Coast, Ken Kesey and his Merry Pranksters introduced novices to the drug in their so-called 'Acid Tests' parties, where the Grateful Dead (then known as the Warlocks) were the house band.

Ex-Harvard lecturer Dr Timothy Leary was an enthusiastic advocate of the drug, while underground chemist Owsley Stanley (the Grateful Dead's soundman) manufactured it. Its mind-altering properties contributed to a blossoming of innovative new musical statements during the period, including the Beatles' *Sgt. Pepper's Lonely Hearts Club Band*, the Jimi Hendrix Experience's breathtaking opening salvo of releases, and the Doors' debut album. Artists spent longer crafting their work, and albums assumed greater artistic validity: in 1968, LP sales overtook those of singles for the first time.

If youth culture at large was promoting peace and love, the wider world hadn't got the message. In 1966, police invoked a curfew on youths on Los Angeles' Sunset Strip, provoking riots and inspiring Buffalo Springfield's understated and balanced 'For What It's Worth'. The year 1967 saw race-related riots in several US cities, including LA (centred on the Watts district) and Detroit; the growing unrest facilitated the rise of the Black Power movement. Major artists such as James Brown ('Say it Loud – I'm Black and I'm Proud'), Aretha Franklin ('Respect') and Nina Simone ('To be Young, Gifted and Black') put forward empowering messages.

In May of the following year, students in Paris took to the streets – ill-feeling between students and Charles de Gaulle's authoritarian government had been brewing for some time. Clashes with gendarmes erupted, resulting in the worst violence in the city's streets for 30 years. Within days, there were mass protests and a general strike by some 10 million workers. Meanwhile, in Czechoslovakia, a brief flowering of political liberalization (the 'Prague Spring') was crushed by Soviet and Warsaw Pact forces.

America lost Dr Martin Luther King Jr and the presidential candidate Robert Kennedy within three months of each other in 1968, both to assassins' bullets. US military fatalities in Vietnam peaked that year, with 16,600 deaths, though South Vietnamese forces lost around 11,000 more. Taken from that year's *Beggars Banquet* – the Rolling Stones' resounding return to form after their mis-step into psychedelia – 'Street Fighting Man' and 'Sympathy for the Devil' tapped into the volatile zeitgeist.

The US landed a man on the Moon on 20 July 1969. Less than a month later, Woodstock Music and Art Fair marked the apex of the hippie era, but the nadir swiftly followed: during a fractious Stones concert at Altamont Speedway in December, a fan was murdered by Hells Angels. And the conflict in Vietnam dragged on, something that informed both Edwin Starr's 'War' and Marvin Gaye's pivotal state-of-our-union address, *What's Going On* (see p.96).

In 1972, five White House operatives were caught carrying out a burglary at the Democratic National Committee HQ in Washington, DC, which had previously also been secretly wiretapped. The resulting 'Watergate' scandal brought down Republican President Richard M. Nixon, who became the first US leader to resign in 1974. The period's conspiracy movies reflected a growing suspicion of government, notably *The Parallax View* (1974), *Three Days of the Condor* (1975) and *All the President's Men* (1976 – based on the Watergate investigations). Early 1970s cinema also saw the rise of so-called Blaxploitation movies, which gave Black Americans long-overdue prominence, and incorporated a handful of exemplary soundtracks by the likes of Isaac Hayes (*Shaft*), Curtis Mayfield (*Superfly*) and Marvin Gaye (*Trouble Man*).

In the UK, an economic crisis precipitated unemployment for public sector workers and the young in the early 1970s. Trades unions – then a major political force – launched strikes in protest, and when miners went on strike for higher pay, the government imposed a three-day working week to conserve energy, as well as ending TV broadcasts at 10.30pm. There were power cuts, nonetheless, prompting unwanted candlelit dinners. Racial discrimination was on the rise too, with the emergence of the right-wing National Front. An atmosphere ripe for punk rock, then.

'YOU CANNOT CHANGE MINDS BY HANDING A FLOWER TO SOME BOZO WHO WANTS TO SHOOT YOU.'

'MOE' TUCKER,
VELVET UNDERGROUND DRUMMER

1967
→   Israel clashes with Palestine in the Yom Kippur War.
→   The Monterey Pop Festival is staged. The first major rock festival, it features notable performances by Jimi Hendrix, Janis Joplin and Big Brother, Otis Redding and the Who.
→   The Beatles release the epochal *Sgt. Pepper's Lonely Hearts Club Band*.
→   Aretha Franklin's 'Respect' is released, going on to become a civil-rights and feminist anthem.

1968
→   Charismatic civil rights leader Martin Luther King Jr is assassinated in Memphis, Tennessee. Two months later, Robert Kennedy – brother of the late US president – is himself gunned down in Los Angeles, California.
→   Student riots in Paris escalate into a national strike and are followed by similar protests in Germany and Italy.
→   Premiere of *2001: A Space Odyssey*, directed by Stanley Kubrick.
→   King Tubby works on early dub releases in Jamaica.

1969
→   In July, Neil Armstrong becomes the first man to walk on the Moon.
→   Launch of IRA terrorist campaign against the UK.
→   The Woodstock festival takes place on a farm in New York State.
→   The Who release the celebrated concept album *Tommy*.

1970
→   Black Sabbath's eponymous debut album lays down the template for heavy metal.

1971
→   Eastern Pakistan separates from its western counterpart, becoming Bangladesh.
→   Steve Reich composes *Drumming*
→   Intel's 4004 becomes the first commercially available microprocessor.
→   George Harrison organizes the Concert for Bangladesh, a charity event to raise funds for war refugees.
→   Stanley Kubrick's controversial, sexually explicit movie *A Clockwork Orange* is released. After several violent crimes apparently inspired by the film, Kubrick withdraws it in the UK.
→   *Shaft*, featuring a Grammy Award-winning soundtrack by Isaac Hayes, becomes one of the earliest and most significant 'Blaxploitation' movies.

1972

→ Philips produces the first VCR (video cassette recorder).

→ The soundtrack for *The Harder They Come* provides an international calling card for reggae.

→ Release of Francis Ford Coppola's *The Godfather*.

1973

→ The Wailers release their breakthrough album *Catch a Fire*.

→ Thomas Pynchon publishes *Gravity's Rainbow*.

→ The Stooges release the proto-punk *Raw Power*.

→ The New York Dolls combine glam rock and punk on their influential eponymous debut album.

1974

→ In the wake of the Watergate scandal, President Richard M. Nixon becomes the first US president in history to resign.

→ In August, the Ramones make their first appearance at New York's CBGB club.

1975

→ Bill Gates and Paul Allen found Microsoft.

→ Release of *Jaws*, widely cited as the first blockbuster movie.

1976

→ The Damned release the first UK punk single, 'New Rose'.

→ Release of the Ramones' self-titled debut album.

→ Steve Jobs, Steve Wozniak and Ronald Wayne found Apple.

NEW YORK ART BRUT

THE VELVET UNDERGROUND & NICO
THE VELVET UNDERGROUND & NICO
1967

If it were a book, it might be Baudelaire's *Les Fleurs du Mal*, or John Rechy's *City of Night* – dissolute, strung-out, beauty with a bite. It's *Sgt. Pepper*'s darker twin – less welcoming but just as revolutionary. Maybe more so.

Contradictions abound. An unknown group with a provocative Pop Art cover – by Andy Warhol, no less. A glum garage band fronted by an arrestingly beautiful model. High and low culture mashed together. Guitars being mugged cheek-by-jowl with a decorous celeste.

Pretty songs. And songs that don't get played on the radio. Take 'Heroin', a drug addict's narrative that surges from delicate arpeggios to a whirling gale. Or 'Venus in Furs', a paean to sado-masochism underpinned by the sinister thrum of an electric viola. Or 'I'm Waiting for the Man', the tale of a drug score set to a hammering, two-chord piano riff. Or 'European Son', a near-eight-minute workout flecked with shards of feedback and the sound of glass smashing.

There's a foretaste of punk in the subject matter, and in the guitar playing of Lou Reed and Sterling Morrison, which eschews showcasing for simplicity: chugging chords and spiky solos. And nothing could be more primal than Maureen 'Moe' Tucker's pounding drums, throbbing like a migraine on 'Heroin'. Tucker played standing up, with mallets and on a stripped-down kit of bass drum, snare and toms. But the first track on *The Velvet Underground & Nico* is 'Sunday Morning', a warm duvet of sound (although ostensibly its subject is paranoia), while 'I'll Be Your Mirror' is disarmingly open-hearted.

Those odd marriages stemmed partly from the Velvets' disparate inspirations. Reed honed his pop sensibilities as a staff writer for Pickwick music publishers, writing off-kilter non-hits such as 'The Ostrich', named for a fictitious dance craze and credited to the Primitives. But like Bob Dylan before him, he brought an expansive love of literature to bear on his lyrics. Reed admired William Burroughs and Nelson Algren, chroniclers of outsiders – addicts, prostitutes, failed lives – and in 1987 summed up his motivation as 'to bring the sensitivities of the novel to rock music'. 'European Son' is dedicated to the poet Delmore Schwartz, who had mentored Reed during his studies at Syracuse University. Among his evocative vignettes here are the cold siren of 'Femme Fatale', a song riddled with snarky put-downs, and the uptight bohemian of 'All Tomorrow's Parties', based on the clique at Warhol's New York studio, the Factory, where the group rehearsed.

Reed also admired Ornette Coleman's improvisatory explorations, but the Velvets' edgiest avant-garde contributions came from John Cale. The Welshman had played piano on a marathon recital of Eric Satie's *Vexations* at New York's

Savage beauty in silhouette: (left to right) John Cale, Nico, Andy Warhol and whip-wielding dancer Gerard Malanga, circa 1966

'WE WERE TRYING TO DO A PHIL SPECTOR THING WITH AS FEW INSTRUMENTS AS POSSIBLE.'

JOHN CALE

Pocket Theatre in 1963, organized by John Cage, the embodiment of a musical open mind ('[Cage] gives you a sheet with dots and diagrams, and gives you the freedom to play what you'd like'). Cale had played amplified viola in La Monte Young's Dream Syndicate too, where he learned to sustain mesmerizing drones for hours on end – a bedrock of the Velvets' sound here – alongside a Minimalist devotion to repetition. Nowhere is the latter heard to greater effect than on 'All Tomorrow's Parties'– Warhol's favourite Velvets song. Cale's playing on a prepared piano (pioneered by Cage) is a Minimalist jackhammer, the song's pounding heart and its weight. Nico only sings lead on three songs – this one being her finest – partly because the other Velvets weren't happy that Warhol had summarily dropped her on them, to up the group's glamour content. But her sombre, deep intonation contributes greatly to the set's dark beauty.

The Velvets stood apart even from the counterculture of the times, particularly the West Coast scene (the Jefferson Airplane and Grateful Dead). They were speed and heroin to the hippie hash and LSD, and their debut album neither looks nor sounds like those of its peers. The myth persists that *The Velvet Underground & Nico* sold zilch; in fact, it shifted nearly 58,500 copies Stateside in the first two years – respectable for a cult band, especially given the abject promotion and distribution by their label, MGM. And anyway, if no one had heard it, it couldn't have become such a crucial influence on what came after, from Jonathan Richman through punk, no wave, R.E.M., the Jesus & Mary Chain (who look like the Velvets' children) and beyond.

In the mid-1960s, forward-thinking minds began alchemizing pop music into something altogether stranger. LSD/acid propelled that change. The explosive sound world of the Beatles' 'Tomorrow Never Knows', from *Revolver* (1966), featured treated vocals, backwards guitar and tape loops. Or the Yardbirds' uneasy 'Happening Ten Years Time Ago', whose explosive middle section sets nagging police sirens against jagged guitar solos.

Music mimicked acid's effects – senses heightened, time and sound distorted. Texan garage band 13th Floor Elevators were among acid's earliest evangelists, an amplified electric jug injecting a disorientating throb. LA's the Doors blended dark poetry with jazz-like excursions. Live, Britain's Pink Floyd improvised at length, though their debut *The Piper at the Gates of Dawn* also incorporated concise, imaginative songs by guitarist Syd Barrett. Childhood and its literature fed into the psych zeitgeist too: that LP's title was a nod to *The Wind in the Willows*, while the Beatles ('Lucy in the Sky with Diamonds'), Jefferson Airplane ('White Rabbit') and others referenced Lewis Carroll's 'Alice' books. The innocence and wonder inherent in the Beach Boys' *Pet Sounds* (1966) and 'Good Vibrations' was the result of time-consuming studio experimentation and complex arrangements.

Non-Western scales and Indian instrumentation – both authentic (the Beatles' 'Within You, Without You') and approximated (the Byrds' 'Eight Miles High') – enriched the sonic palette. The Yardbirds incorporated Gregorian chant and disorienting guitar breaks on 'Happenings Ten Years Time Ago', while Jimi Hendrix merged guitar wizardry with studio innovations on his debut album and genre milestones such as 'Purple Haze' and 'All Along the Watchtower'.

A TROPICÁLIA ONE-OFF

OS MUTANTES
OS MUTANTES
1968

São Paulo's Os Mutantes comprised two brothers – Sérgio Dias Baptista and his brother Arnaldo – with singer Rita Lee, then Arnaldo's girlfriend. All were young when they made this record, but as Sérgio told *Shindig!* in 2016, that fed into its invigorating *joie de vivre*. 'We had no fear and freedom is simply not to be afraid; afraid to love, to confront, to try the new, to experiment.'

The abundance of ideas on the album can be bewildering, scattershot even, but for unbridled energy and inventiveness it had few peers, even in the heady late 60s. No one track defines it, nor prepares you for what you'll hear next. *Sgt. Pepper* and psychedelia were touchstones, but so were *musique concrète*, Italian and French pop and home-grown genres such as bossa nova.

Opener 'Panis et Circenses' sets the out-there tone: having played for around two minutes, it slows to a stop, then abruptly resumes, only to cease once more; cutlery clatters and we appear to be listening in on a coffee break. But there are perfectly concise nuggets of garage pop here too, from a joyful take on Gilberto Gil and Caetano Veloso's 'Bat Macumba', propelled by samba drums, to the psych delights of Jorge Ben's 'A Minha Menina', its hook played on electric guitar via a homemade fuzzbox. (It was memorably covered by the Bees on their 2002 debut album.) The voices in 'O Relógio' and a cover of Françoise Hardy's 'Le Premier Bonheur du Jour' are straight out of the easy-listening songbook, but even a straightforward bossa nova such as 'Adeus, Maria Fulô' features a *musique concrète*-style intro and hand drums doubling as a bass.

Os Mutantes is a landmark release in the story of Tropicália, the countercultural movement that became a rallying point for anti-establishment feeling in the aftermath of Brazil's violent coup d'état in 1964, and the oppressive military rule that followed. Censorship was rife and dissent wasn't tolerated (both Gil and Veloso were put under house arrest, then forced into exile). Issued the same year as this album, the AI-5 Act clamped down on any music deemed subversive, among a host of other repressive restrictions. All of which adds an extra dimension to an anarchic record that shirks musical conservatism in favour of freeform innovation – a subtle political statement in itself.

Thirty years later, Os Mutantes were rediscovered by the likes of David Byrne and Beck. The latter's 1998 *Mutations* nods to the band in its name and the track 'Tropicália', while the title of Byrne's Os Mutantes compilation *Everything is Possible!* is this album's credo in a nutshell.

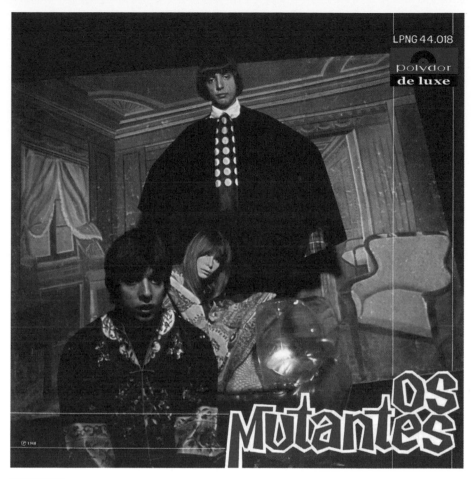

Mutant genius

FRENCH FREE VERSE MEETS WORLD MUSIC

COMME À LA RADIO
BRIGITTE FONTAINE
1969

By the time she released her debut album (1968's *Brigitte Fontaine est... folle!*), Fontaine was already an accomplished actress and playwright. That set bore the hallmarks of French chanson, with lush orchestrations by future Serge Gainsbourg collaborator Jean-Claude Vannier. But this sophomore release marks a vault into unexplored territory.

Invaluable contributions come from her artistic allies: songwriter Jacques Higelin, a leftfield folk songwriter, and the Berber composer/multi-instrumentalist/actor Areski Belkacem. The three collaborated on theatrical productions around this time, in which non-Western sonorities (African, Arabic) bubbled and pulsed beneath Fontaine's recitations. To that tantalizing mélange, the trio added US avant-garde jazz troupe the Art Ensemble of Chicago.

'Tanka I' enters on a shower of lute and zither notes, Belkacem and Fontaine's vocals criss-crossing (the title references a form of short Japanese lyric poetry). 'L'été l'été' interweaves a sopranino saxophone, trumpet, lute and zither, creating a dreamlike, buzzing texture against which Belkacem and Fontaine's voices play: hers deliciously enunciated; his more rhythmic, like a tolling reminder of time passing. For the most part, 'Tanka II' pairs the most unsettling of love songs with Belkacem's beguiling hand-drum patters and lithe snippets of bass from the Ensemble's Malachi Favors, before abruptly giving way to a cryptic spoken coda that references Marx.

The title track is an eight-minute dance between Fontaine's low, soft vocals, staccato interjections from trumpet and flute, and a pared-down Favors bass line. Her free-verse poetry, which may sound disarmingly charming to the ear of the non-French speaker, is anything but: two cops pull a wounded youth from an ambulance and tip him into a river; dogs are run over; an elderly drunk is incapacitated beneath her bed. Perspective shifts from abstract observation to sharply focused scenarios and back again.

Each track is a soundscape unto itself, heavy with ethnic ambience – indeed, this was one of the earliest sets to introduce textures from so-called world music to a French audience. Even the mix is unconventional, with percussion to the fore, and other instruments to the rear – distant, sometimes strained.

A mysterious, singular release that exists in a space apart from its peers and of its time.

comme à la radio

Brigitte Fontaine: *radio* drama

REVOLUTION FROM STUDIO TO STREET 1967–1976

ANTHEM FOR A DIVIDED NATION

'THE STAR-SPANGLED BANNER' AT WOODSTOCK FESTIVAL
JIMI HENDRIX
1969

By the time Hendrix took the stage at the Woodstock Festival on 18 August 1969, most of the 300,000-plus crowd had dispersed. No matter. In less than four minutes, he created an unparalleled commentary on one of his country's defining conflicts.

He'd first played 'The Star-Spangled Banner' the previous year, and would still be revisiting it in 1970, the year of his death. That ongoing dialogue doubtless reflected the guitarist's complex attitudes to his national anthem and what it represented. Not least to Black Americans, who were still discriminated against in the wake of the 1964 Civil Rights Act and had seen two of their most inspirational leaders (Malcolm X and Martin Luther King Jr) assassinated inside three years, along with Robert Kennedy, the supportive US Attorney General and presidential candidate gunned down two months after King.

Hendrix is true to the notes of the original melody (taken from a tune by British composer John Stafford Smith), but it's as if the clear vision embodied in its lyrics – by Francis Scott Key – is periodically obscured. Clouds of distortion blow in, like the smoke from the fires that had consumed US cities that decade, or the tear gas employed to dispel rioters, or burning Vietnamese jungles. Dive-bomb effects punctuate the music. High, shrieking notes could be bullets keening through the air, or victims' cries (this music has something of Picasso's 1937 canvas *Guernica* about it). A snippet of 'The Last Post' cuts through; with the Vietnam War at its zenith, the context was plain.

But it ends with something like triumph, a rapid surge of rising chords. Hendrix had served in the 101st Airborne Division, though he was discharged, and clearly felt a kinship with servicemen in action – unlike most of his hippie audience that day in upstate New York. So was this an implicit comment on them too? Like all great art, Hendrix's performance invites multiple interpretations. This is not a straightforward demolition of America's national anthem and what it stands for; indeed, when chat-show host Dick Cavett referred to Hendrix's radical reading of it, the guitarist replied, 'I thought it was beautiful, but there you go.' (He sounded harder a year later at LA's Forum, prefacing another take on 'The Star-Spangled Banner' by alluding to 'the home of the pigs and the violence of the Black Panthers'.)

Fifty years later, in the era of Childish Gambino's 'This is America' and the Black Lives Matter movement (see p.192), Hendrix's 'Star-Spangled Banner' remains depressingly relevant.

Fringe festival: Jimi closes out Woodstock

REVOLUTION FROM STUDIO TO STREET 1967–1976

MUSIC AND THE VIETNAM WAR

America's protracted and controversial struggle in Vietnam inspired abundant musical comment, from both sides of the political divide. Victor Lundberg's US Top 10 hit 'An Open Letter to My Teenage Son' (1967) – recited against the Civil War-era 'Battle Hymn of the Republic' – piled on the guilt in the form of a father disowning his draft-dodging offspring. Taken from a flag-waving John Wayne movie of the same year, and performed by its composer Staff Sergeant Barry Sadler, 'The Ballad of the Green Berets' did even better, topping the *Billboard* chart for five weeks in spring 1966, shifting 9-million-plus copies and becoming that year's bestselling single Stateside.

Fewer, but perhaps more interesting, are those tracks that saw both sides of the argument. Kenny Rogers and the First Edition's 'Ruby, Don't Take Your Love to Town' isn't explicitly tied to one conflict, but its tale of a battle-crippled vet and his errant wife carried serious emotional heft in the Vietnam era. Jimi Hendrix's performance of 'The Star-Spangled Banner' (see previous pages) could be read neither as all-out attack nor patriotic salute, but an uneasy conversation between the two. George Crumb's three-movement *Black Angels* is an avant-garde composition written for an all-electric string quartet. Completed on Friday, 13 March 1970 and inscribed '*in tempore belli*', its nightmarish and surreal soundscape (water-filled crystal glasses also feature), like those of Hendrix, act as eloquent wordless testament to the confusion and horror of the period.

John Fogerty of Creedence Clearwater Revival reminisced to *Rolling Stone*, 'In 1968, the majority of the country thought morale was great among the troops, and eighty percent of them were in favor of the war.' That said, a creeping realization was dawning on many Americans that this war, the grounds for which were debatable at best, might also be unwinnable. Fogerty's 'Fortunate Son' – while sympathetic to troops on the ground – deplored the fact that wealthy citizens could step in to prevent their offspring from seeing action, an option not open to poorer parents.

Of course, if you happened to be fighting in a Vietnamese forest, songs you knew from home took on new dimensions – binding you to what you'd left, and to your fellow soldiers in the field. Doug Bradley and Craig Werner interviewed a host of war veterans about which songs meant most to them for their 2015 book *We Gotta Get Out of this Place*. The song that inspired its title was hugely popular, for obvious reasons, but other favourites included Porter Wagoner's misty-eyed 'Green, Green Grass of Home' and Jimi Hendrix's 'Purple Haze' – its sonic arsenal evoking chattering guns and whirling chopper blades; smoke grenades gave off purple smoke too.

And Former Navy serviceman Joseph Allen 'Country Joe' McDonald's 'I-Feel-Like-I'm-Fixin'-to-Die Rag', whose sentiment chimed strongly with men unsure why they were where they were, and what the fighting was for anyway. 'It's military humor that only a soldier could get away with,' McDonald told Bradley and Werner. 'It comes out of a tradition of GI humor in which people can bitch in a way that will not get them in trouble but keeps them from insanity.'

'I'M A VETERAN FIRST AND A HIPPIE SECOND.'

'COUNTRY JOE' McDONALD

A REBIRTH OF CLUB CULTURE

DAVID MANCUSO OPENS THE LOFT
1970

Before disco became the mainstream, it was underground, polymorphous, inclusive. And much of its alluring ethos was down to David Mancuso.

On Valentine's Day 1970, Mancuso staged the first of a series of invitation-only parties at his apartment at 647 Broadway, in downtown Manhattan's then down-at-heel warehouse district. There was juice, punch, fruit and sweets. Balloons and streamers festooned the ceiling. The crowd was largely gay and multiracial (unusual for the time), but with a high female contingent too. Mancuso carefully curated the music so that it ebbed and flowed, peaked and receded and built again, sustaining a vibe all night. The audiophile sound system, developed with electronics expert Alex Rosner, gave warm and detailed reproduction, the volume deliberately pitched so that the dancers had to attune their ears and listen. Not just a party, but a welcoming, non-judgemental communal environment. And Mancuso as host, not superstar DJ: 'I'm just part of the vibration,' he insisted to *The Wire*'s Tim Lawrence in 2007. 'I want to feel a sense of camaraderie.' He abhorred the kind of exclusivity that later made clubs such as Studio 54, in downtown New York, so hard to get in to.

Mancuso had adored psychedelic music, taken readily to acid (with which the punch at the Loft was reportedly spiked) and still adhered to the optimism and universality of the previous decade's 'love generation'. That openness also informed the Loft's thrillingly diverse music, from James Brown funk to Chicago's cover of 'I'm a Man' to the uplifting *Missa Luba* mass sung by a Congolese male-voice choir. Such was Mancuso's burgeoning influence that after he seized on the infectiously funky import single 'Soul Makossa' by Cameroonian saxophonist Manu Dibango, it took off, gaining heavy airplay on the city's top Black radio station, inspiring multiple cover versions, reaching No.35 on the *Billboard* chart, and later filtering into Michael Jackson's iconic hit 'Wanna Be Startin' Somethin''.

The Loft offered a template that many of the era's defining clubs – the Gallery, Soho Place, Paradise Garage, the Warehouse – assimilated and adapted. Its enlightened environment attracted the likes of Frankie Knuckles, Larry Levan and François Kevorkian, through whom disco became house music. Something of the Loft's atmosphere of collective transcendence resurfaced in acid house, rave and pretty much all modern dance music in its heterogeneous glory. After all, invites for that first party in 1970 bore the legend 'Love Saves the Day'.

Eyes to the Loft: disco godfather David Mancuso in 1974

REVOLUTION FROM STUDIO TO STREET 1967–1976

DISCO AND THE RISE OF THE DJ

In the early 1970s, David Mancuso and Francis Grasso (who played at New York's the Sanctuary) began to transform the DJ's role, creatively tailoring their sets for an audience. Society's marginalized groups – LGBTQ, but also Black and Latino communities – found solace and escapism in their clubs.

Feeding off the energy that the Sanctuary's gay clientele brought with them, Grasso dispensed with the vibe-killing gaps between spins by segueing tracks. Using headphones, he'd line up the next record while the current one was still on the turntable, 'beat mixing' so that the rhythm and tempo of one crossed seamlessly into that of its successor, like a relay baton. That hunger for a continuous dance experience also inspired DJs to create extended mixes by alternating between two copies of the same record, fostering an immersive environment and marathon-length sets.

In 1972, maverick talent Tom Moulton hit on the idea of making his own 45-minute dance tape, by painstakingly cutting and splicing together hit songs; it took him 80 hours. By 1975, he had created a flowing 18-minute megamix for the opening two songs on Gloria Gaynor's *Never Can Say Goodbye* LP; by speeding up the tempo, enhancing the sound using an equalizer, and inserting drum breaks, he refashioned the original versions. That same year, Moulton performed a mix of Al Downing's 'I'll Be Holding On', but when he took it to be mastered, only 12-inch blank metal discs were available. By happy accident, he discovered that the sound quality was far richer and more dynamic than it would have been as a 7-inch: the first 12-inch single had arrived.

Contemporaneously, reggae pioneers (see p.104 onwards) were evolving dub, whose techniques would lend themselves to remixing, but disco DJs were on a parallel path. In 1976, the Salsoul label commissioned Walter Gibbons to remix Double Exposure's 'Ten Percent', in what became the first commercially available 12-inch single (Moulton's 'I'll Be Holding On' wasn't released until later). The following year, he performed an even more audacious reworking of

Proto DJ superstar Larry Levan on the decks at the Paradise Garage, 1978

Loleatta Holloway's 'Hit and Run' after being given the song's multitrack tapes, allowing him to drastically reshape the original.

Disco went into sharp decline in the late 1970s, but by then, ex-Loft habitués (and friends since childhood) Larry Levan and Frankie Knuckles were already germinating what Knuckles famously dubbed 'disco's revenge': house music. Levan's performances at the Paradise Garage took in everything from punk and new wave to Motown and Afro-Cuban music, and were programmed according to theme or emotion, guiding the audience on a journey. A worshipful following dubbed them 'Saturday Mass'. Levan was also one of the era's finest producers and remixers, employing techniques learned from dub – witness his mixes of 'I Got My Mind Made up' by Instant Funk, and Smokey Robinson's 'And I Don't Love You'.

Frankie Knuckles played similarly eclectic sets – often including Euro synth pop alongside R&B and disco – at Chicago's Warehouse and Music Box clubs, using a Pioneer reel-to-reel tape machine to edit, loop, rearrange and extend tracks. Sometime around 1983, he began overlaying raw electro pulses from a rhythm box, and later a Roland 909 drum machine, to his sets, creating classic Chicago house. Both men were revered. The cult of the DJ had arrived.

TRUE METAL'S FIRST MASTERPIECE

PARANOID
BLACK SABBATH
1970

Their eponymous debut LP, released just seven months before this (on a Friday the 13th, naturally), invented heavy metal: doom-laden name (inspired by a Boris Karloff flick at their local cinema), creepy cover art, bludgeoning riffs, and all opening with the sound of a bell tolling against a thunderous background. But with *Paranoid*, Black Sabbath took metal overground, into the charts and the public consciousness for the first time. *Paranoid* made No.1 on the UK album charts. It made Sabbath, too.

Fellow volume merchants Led Zeppelin and Deep Purple were honing a blues-derived hard rock. But unlike them, Sabbath weren't singing about heartache or sex. Rather, *Paranoid* brims over with nihilism and desperation, something encapsulated in its title track – the sound of a terrified man that also gave them a UK No.4. Ozzy Osbourne's whine doesn't have the range, power or testosterone levels of Led Zep's Robert Plant or Purple's Ian Gillan, but convincingly channels the track's wide-eyed angst while the power trio behind him hammer monolithically (and atypically quickly) through a chord cycle, with staccato downstrokes from guitarist Tony Iommi, making them sound not unlike a punk band. (In 1978, the Ramones opened for them on a US tour.)

'War Pigs' is more emblematic of early Sabbath, though: an anti-war song, air-raids already moaning in its opening seconds, whose original lyrics were rewritten after the group realized they might reinforce their unwanted devil-worshipping image. Spitting riffs and the bleakest imagery combine in an anthem for the Vietnam years (bassist Geezer Butler once quipped that warmongering politicians were the true Satanists). For Sabbath, there are man-made horrors aplenty on Earth without descending into hell. 'Hand of Doom' dealt with returning Vietnam vets strung out on heroin, 'Electric Funeral' with life after an atomic armageddon, with a further apocalyptic scenario on 'Iron Man', Iommi's slab-like riff providing another blueprint for future metalheads to study. The mask slips but once, on the folky ode to space travel, 'Planet Caravan'.

Sabbath's role in the birth of a new genre went unheralded by most critics. *Rolling Stone*'s Lester Bangs championed 60s garage bands for their primal urgency, but deemed Sabbath 'unskilled laborers' and 'Just like Cream! But worse.' Of *Paranoid*, Robert Christgau retrospectively offered the patronizing 'I suppose I could enjoy them as camp, like a horror movie,' along with a C-rating. US radio DJs and programmers were similarly snobbish. *Paranoid* received barely any airplay, but still made No.12 Stateside.

Sabbath on the *Never Say Die* tour, London's Hammersmith Odeon, 1978

All of Sabbath were from poor, working-class stock and weren't impressed by hippie escapism or hollow dreams of a loved-up shared utopia. They weren't golden-maned rock gods and they weren't going to sing about stairways to heaven; their hellish visions were inspired in part by the stultifying dead-end streets of their upbringing in post-industrial Birmingham. That may have made them unfashionable among rock's cognoscenti, but it earned them legions of fans.

That these songs weren't graced with prog-rock curlicues, glowing harmonies or enigmatic Dylanesque couplets was beside the point; there's a taut focus to Sabbath's sonic onslaught on *Paranoid*, epitomized by Iommi's playing. Famously, he accidentally cut off two fingertips while filling in for a sheet-metal cutter at a factory (ironically, he'd been planning to quit that day). He fashioned some homemade prosthetic replacements, but the event also forced him to use lighter-gauge strings and simplify his guitar playing as certain chords were now too tricky to finger. And as for 'unskilled laborers' – well, Sabbath weren't averse to meter changes, jazz excursions, improvisation or even swing.

Later releases perfected the formula. On follow-up *Master of Reality*, Iommi began concertedly drop-tuning his strings, making them looser and thus easier on his damaged fingers. By lowering their pitch, he also generated a thicker, sludgier sound (one that became an enduring characteristic of doom metal and stoner rock) – especially when bassist Butler followed suit.

But that came next. It was *Paranoid* that kicked the door down.

'WE ARRIVED AT THE HEIGHT OF THE VIETNAM WAR AND ON THE OTHER SIDE OF THE HIPPIE ERA, SO THERE WAS A MOOD OF DOOM AND AGGRESSION.'

GEEZER BUTLER

Tousled curls and twin necks: Led Zep's Plant and Page

Metal was forged by Black Sabbath in Birmingham, whose environs – steel mills, factories, industry at its heaviest – resonated with pounding noise. The West Midlands also spawned Robert Plant and John Bonham of Led Zeppelin, whose blues-inspired hard rock formed a second prong in the (un)Holy Trinity of Metal. Once Deep Purple exchanged orchestras and prog-rock for riffery and swagger (epitomized by 'Strange Kind of Woman', 'Highway Star' or 'Black Night'), they became the third.

Topped off with Lemmy's sandpaper-throated vocals, Motörhead shared a musical affinity with punk (he briefly subbed on bass with the Damned), and were a direct influence on 80s speed and thrash metal. With their *British Steel* LP, Birmingham's Judas Priest recalibrated metal at the turn of the decade, helping to kickstart 80s thrash metal. Their twin-axe attack and singer Rob Halford's operatic-style delivery impacted directly on the cumbersomely titled New Wave of British Heavy Metal, encompassing younger bands such as Iron Maiden and Def Leppard, to whom punk was a core inspiration.

Metal's milestones had been mostly made in Britain. Van Halen – who, symbolically, upstaged Black Sabbath as a support act on their 1978 tour – redressed the balance with their debut set the following year, highlighted by guitarist Eddie Van Halen's eye-popping tapping skills. 'Listen to the first Van Halen album,' Leppard's Joe Elliott told *MOJO* in 2007. 'It was time for a clean sweep, a tighter version of rock.'

ONE MAN'S STATE-OF-THE-UNION ADDRESS

WHAT'S GOING ON
MARVIN GAYE
1971

Marvin Gaye was disillusioned both with his own success and his risk-averse label, Motown. What price a *Billboard* hit against a background of US involvement in a protracted war abroad, violent unrest back home and the environment in freefall? This was his response.

Curtis Mayfield had penned affirmative, socially engaged songs such as 'People Get Ready', but *What's Going On* went further: a concept protest album in the form of an integrated suite, by a Black American artist. Unprecedentedly for Motown, Gaye also produced it, having proved himself on hits by vocal group the Originals. Working with them, he discovered possibilities for layering and interweaving his own voice, part of *What's Going On*'s distinctive sound. In another first for the label, the lyrics would be printed and the musicians credited.

The title track originated with in-house writer Al Cleveland and the Four Tops' Renaldo 'Obie' Benson, though Gaye refined it. Motown's boss Berry Gordy Jr was reluctant to release a single so heavy with social commentary, dubbing it 'the worst thing I ever heard in my life'. But it soared to No.2 on the pop listings, selling 100,000 copies on day one. An album had to follow, one that would pick up on the jazzy, easy flow of that track, the vocals laid-back and conversational.

Discussions with his brother Frankie, a Vietnam vet, supplied the framework for the songs: a returning soldier taking stock of his America. What does he find? Nature degraded ('Mercy Mercy Me [the Ecology]') and heroin rife in US ghettos ('Flyin' High [in the Friendly Sky]'). 'Inner City Blues (Make Me Wanna Holler)' focuses on urban deprivation and anguish, suggesting money for the Space Race could ease the lives of countless poverty-stricken Black Americans – 'Whitey's on the Moon', as Gil Scott-Heron's 1970 poem had it. For Gaye, ultimate comfort and redemption can only lie in spiritual faith. 'God is writing this album,' he once told Smokey Robinson. 'God is working through me.'

These weren't pop topics, and their setting wasn't pop either. Tenor saxophone underpins much of the mix, adding jazzy undertones, while David Van DePitte's arrangements expanded on Gaye's fragmentary song sketches. But it made sense as a new kind of soul album for tough times – and it swiftly found an audience, becoming his career bestseller.

Public Enemy rage over manic sound collages, demanding to be heard. *What's Going On* draws the listener in on smooth grooves and mellifluous vocals, hard politics softly spoken.

Soul of a nation: Gaye sings the changes in the early 70s

REVOLUTION FROM STUDIO TO STREET 1967–1976

A NABOKOVIAN CULT CLASSIC

HISTOIRE DE MELODY NELSON
SERGE GAINSBOURG
1971

A pubescent English girl is knocked off her bike by a middle-aged Frenchman in his Rolls-Royce. He deflowers her in a hotel, but later the homesick girl flies back to her native Sunderland. The plane crashes, pulled down by sorcerers so that a cargo cult may harvest its wreckage. *Histoire de Melody Nelson* tells the story in seven songs and with a running time of just 28 minutes – a *Lolita*-esque symphonic-rock hybrid concept album that remains Gainsbourg's finest hour.

He'd met future paramour Jane Birkin on a film set in 1968, and later gifted her a leather-bound book of his lyrics, with an inscription pledging to write *Melody Nelson* for her. Birkin would go on to sing Melody's part and appear on the album's cover, bewigged and freckled, but in 1968, Gainsbourg only had a title.

He considered English session musicians superior to those in his native France, and came to the Philips studio in London's Marble Arch to record. In semi-improvisatory, free-flowing sessions, they taped louche grooves, highlighted by loose, funky bass. The occasional gritty guitar freak-out are as 'rock' as things get.

Jean-Claude Vannier overlaid lush, graceful string arrangements, adding 'an oriental colour that has never dated' in Birkin's words, along with the swelling choral parts of 'Cargo Culte'. Unconventionally, the tunefulness comes from Vannier's orchestra, as Gainsbourg's vocal is mostly hushed semi-speech, silky and loaded, shivering with expectation and fear on 'L'hôtel Particulier'. Is the listener being seduced into implicitly complying with statutory rape? Or is the entire thing a fantasy (as with Vladimir Nabokov's novel *Lolita*, this is really all about the narrator – an evasively unreliable figure)?

It limped to No.56 in France, selling only around 20,000 copies. But more perceptive critics and fellow musicians recognized *Melody Nelson* as something new and important – a complete song cycle, thematically unified, multiple layers of meaning hidden in its deftly penned, punning lyrics.

It's had a long and influential afterlife, sampled by artists from David Holmes and Massive Attack to Ice T and De La Soul. Beck drew heavily on its musical template for *Sea Change* (2002), while something of its smoky ambience resurfaces in French duo Air (think 'La Femme d'Argent' or 'Playground Love'). But Gainsbourg's original has a svelte sleaze all its own.

At home with the Jane Birkin and Serge Gainsbourg: rue de Verneuil in Paris's 7th arrondissement, December 1971

'IT'S A TRUE ALBUM— ITS TALE OF INNOCENCE LOST AND UNEARNED LAST CHANCES WOULDN'T WORK AS WELL IN ANY OTHER MEDIUM.'

KEITH PHIPPS, *THE A.V. CLUB*

REVOLUTION FROM STUDIO TO STREET 1967–1976

GLAM ROCK'S ORIGINAL ROCK'N'ROLL ALIEN

THE RISE AND FALL OF ZIGGY STARDUST AND THE SPIDERS FROM MARS
DAVID BOWIE
1972

For a while, Bowie seemed a one-hit wonder – that hit being 1969's UK No.5 'Space Oddity'. But by 1974, he could justifiably claim that 'People look to me to see what the spirit of the 70s is.' That dizzying shift came with *Ziggy Stardust*.

The album's plotline is hazy at best (ditto Bowie's next opus, *Diamond Dogs*). But the songs more than make up for any narrative shortfalls, the scorching title track alone neatly encapsulating Ziggy's frantic trajectory. Shades of 1950s rock haunt the apocalyptic 'Five Years' and 'Rock'n'roll Suicide', whose arc from sparse opening to all-guns-blazing finale recalls 1971's epic 'Life on Mars?'. Pile-driving rocker 'Suffragette City' and 'Moonage Daydream' showcase the brilliance of Bowie's guitarist and string arranger, Mick Ronson. 'Starman' – dashed off when the label didn't hear a single – took its signature octave leap at the start of the chorus from 'Somewhere Over the Rainbow', and displays a similar endearing optimism.

The album's commercial impact was emphatic: a UK No.5, with delirious fans packing out concert halls and Ziggymania rampant. Its cultural impact surpassed it, though. Pop rival and former Mod running mate Marc Bolan may have pipped Bowie to become glam's first star, but couldn't match his expansiveness and depth.

Bowie had assimilated theatre and mime alongside Beat writers and the (then little-known) Velvet Underground. Nietzschean super beings – something of a Bowie obsession back then – crop up on 1971's *Hunky Dory*, and the emotional palette he drew on was darker by far than Bolan's, from fears about insanity on *The Man Who Sold the World* (1970) to a doomed Earth sucked dry of resources on *Ziggy Stardust*, while Ziggy and his Spiders wore outfits inspired by the jumpsuits worn by Alex and his Droogs in Stanley Kubrick's 1971 violent sci-fi movie *A Clockwork Orange*. Yet *Ziggy* sold by the bucketful, introducing teenagers to a wealth of cross-cultural references and inspirations.

Even among peers such as Bolan and Roxy Music, Bowie-as-Ziggy stood out. In the famous *Top of the Pops* footage of the group performing 'Starman', he's a spiky-haired androgyne, flopping an arm around Ronson's shoulders and twirling a painted fingernail at the camera. If you were young and gay, or simply unsure where your sexual preferences lay, this registered; even if you weren't, it was provocatively unsettling.

Stardust memories: Ziggy at Hammersmith Odeon, July 1973

AFROBEAT BREAKS OUT

GENTLEMAN
FELA KUTI
1973

'If you want to develop your own sound,' Kraftwerk's Karl Bartos once mused, 'you have to go down new paths or at least change your perspective.' Nigeria's Fela Kuti knew something about that. A gifted multi-instrumentalist and bandleader, he'd toured the USA in the late 1960s, purveying a blend of jazz and African highlife music. But a relationship with ex-Black Panther Sandra Smith opened his eyes to the burgeoning Black Power movement there, leading him to question the music he was making and fostering an outspokenness that only increased over time.

Thereafter, and with the invaluable input of outrageously dextrous drummer Tony Allen, he set about honing a sound and attitude more true to his African heritage. With Afrobeat, Kuti created an enticing blend of polyrhythms, vernacular West African harmonies and call-and-response vocals, jazz, funk and trenchant political observations. In other words, incandescently danceable protest music. Allen remembers members of James Brown's band – *James Brown, no less!* – checking out Kuti's Africa 70 group at the Afro-Spot (Kuti's Lagos club) and noting down his drum patterns.

Shakara (1972) runs it close, but *Gentleman* is probably the first fully formed Afrobeat album and kicked off Kuti's imperial phase. On the 14-and-a-half-minute title track, he asserts his pride in being African, while railing against incipient Westernization. Set up by Kuti's unaccompanied, free-flying saxophone solo, the first half of 'Gentleman' is a mesmerizing workout of horns and itchy syncopated rhythm. When he finally launches into a vocal, it's a sarcastic, broken-English put-down of compatriots still in thrall to colonialist customs, a point reinforced by the comically besuited monkey on the album's cover. It was 12 years after Nigeria broke free from British rule, but for Kuti too many of his fellow citizens had not yet achieved mental independence from their past. The interplay with the backing vocals builds the track's dynamic energy.

Two eight-minute jams ('Fefe Naa Efe' and 'Igbe') present an irresistible blend of punchy horns and complex musical interplay, underpinned by Allen's restless percussion. Funk, but more intricate than its American counterpart. 'Have you ever heard anyone play like me?' Allen asked *MOJO* rhetorically in 2011. 'James Brown's drummer? James Brown's two drummers? No.'

One high-profile fan of Afrobeat was Brian Eno, who recalled his astonishment on hearing Kuti's early 70s work. 'I told the Talking Heads that this was the music of the future and it still is,' he maintained. 'This is what I'd have liked jazz to have become.'

Protest, provocation and polyrhythms: Kuti in 1986 at Orchestra Hall in Detroit, Michigan

'THIS WAS THE MUSIC OF THE FUTURE.'

BRIAN ENO

THE FIRST DUB MASTERPIECE

UPSETTERS 14 DUB BLACKBOARD JUNGLE
LEE 'SCRATCH' PERRY/ UPSETTERS
1973

In the early 70s, instrumental-only LPs, including 1970's *The Undertaker* (Derrick Harriott and the Crystalites) and 1972's *This is Augustus Pablo*, signalled a new direction within reggae. Compilation albums appeared featuring dub mixes that had originally appeared as single B-sides. But the following year, more radically experimental sets were released by the likes of Herman Chin Loy (*Aquarius Dub*) and Lee 'Scratch' Perry. Along with 1974's *Pick a Dub* by Keith Hudson, they represented arrestingly new directions for the genre. But Perry's *Upsetters 14 Dub Blackboard Jungle* stands alone as the first fully formed, thematically unified dub album.

Taking existing rhythm tracks that he'd already produced (and featuring the stellar likes of Wailers Aston 'Family Man' Barrett and his brother Carlton, Augustus Pablo on melodica and Skatalite Tommy McCook), Perry wreaks mighty reinvention. He deconstructs each song, stripping out parts, adding new ones and rebuilding again to create something strange and wonderful – as if they'd made Alice's trip through the looking glass. Emerging on the other side, they aren't so much songs as aural textures, a dizzying new sound world – entirely appropriate for a man whose strongly spiritual nature was run through with mysticism (and who had a robust appetite for ganja).

Drums are surrounded with cavernous reverb. Bass lines become solo stars. Horns echo back from a phantom limboland. Today, the concept of using a recording studio as an instrument in its own right has become worn with overuse, but if the concept is true of Brian Wilson, Phil Spector or Brian Eno, it's assuredly true of Lee 'Scratch' Perry.

Take opener 'Black Panta' – introduced with toasting from Perry himself – which reworks the source 'Bucky Skank' to create a roomy mood piece, hi-hat ticking in the background alongside studio-devised animalistic interjections (perhaps an allusion to the titular jungle) and an odd zipper-like effect (actually a glissando on electric guitar). Junior Byles' mellifluous vocal on 'A Place Called Africa' is replaced by a round and full bass line for 'African Skank', fleeting snatches of a guitar-like landscape glimpsed from a train, drums in a world of echo. 'Elephant Rock' reduces the Hurricanes' 'You Can Run' to a rumbling bedrock of drums and bass, while Prince Django's 'Hot Tip' re-emerges as 'Kasha Macka', on which toasting cedes ground to a hypnotic round of bass line, juddering bass drum and somewhere in the far distance, a lonesome backing vocal. As if to alleviate the intense sonic whirlwind, Perry's idiosyncratic humour

Scratch outside his Black Ark studios in Kingston, Jamaica

REVOLUTION FROM STUDIO TO STREET 1967–1976

weaves the melody of 'Pop Goes the Weasel' into 'Drum Rock' and 'Three Blind Mice' into 'Jungle Jim'. The album's mythic reputation was enhanced by its limited release of 300 (200 of which were set aside for Jamaica) and a 1981 reissue – as *Blackboard Jungle Dub* – with a different track listing and an alternative mix was not universally praised.

Throughout the set, the rhythm sections remain parked on one channel, the brighter treble frequencies of guitars and horns on the other. In this, as in the transmogrifying use of reverb, Perry was constructing new templates for dub. The album was mixed at fellow pioneer Osbourne 'King Tubby' Ruddock's home studio at 18 Dromilly Avenue in Kingston's Waterhouse ghetto. Indeed, Tubby co-mixed the album with Perry, though the extent of his contribution remains somewhat muddied, not least because Perry somewhat muddied it. Reportedly, the two men mixed on separate channels.

The album's after-quakes have resounded down the years – among other things it's an astounding example of what we'd later describe as remixing. Moreover (and allowing for earlier studio wizards such as Les Paul and Joe Meek), with this album Perry more or less defined the concept of producer-as-creative-artist, a hybrid role still being explored today by contemporary cultural figureheads such as Kanye West.

'HE WAS JAMAICA'S SALVADOR DALÍ OF SOUND.'

DON LETTS

A dub benchmark from 1976 whose cast of reggae royalty included the Wailers' Barrett brothers and Robbie Shakespeare

Jamaica had a tradition of producers creating single acetates ('dubplates') of their recordings, for DJs to road-test at sound systems. Legend has it that in 1968, sound-system operator Osbourne 'King Tubby' Redwood and engineer Byron Smith created an instrumental-only dubplate of the Paragons' 'On the Beach'. Played live through Tubby's Hometown Hi-Fi sound system at a dance, with a DJ improvising scats (or 'toasting') over the rhythm, it caused a sensation. Soon, B-sides of singles were given over to instrumental-only 'versions' of the A-side.

Key among dub's leading alchemists was King Tubby, who in the early 70s began adding sudden drop-outs echo, reverb and phasing to versions on a mixing desk in the front room of his Kingston home. Over a core of bass and drums, or bass alone, Tubby added billowing reverb to certain instruments, muting others altogether, while adding high-pass filters that cut out lower frequencies. The classic dub sound was topped off by mastering the recording with heavy compression, making the snare sound explode out of speakers.

THE ROAD TO THE FUTURE

'AUTOBAHN'
KRAFTWERK
1975

As the hypnotic 22-minute-plus title track of their 1974 album, 'Autobahn' took up the whole of the vinyl's side one. But after it attracted airplay in the USA, a three-and-a-half-minute edit was released as a single and, surprisingly, made No.25 on the *Billboard* chart – a first for a German-language song. From Jack Kerouac's novel *On the Road* to 'Route 66', the highway was hard-wired into American culture. Now, a German group had added their own twist.

Nothing before had sounded quite like it. Inspired by long journeys on Germany's iconic motorways, 'Autobahn' incorporated the sound of car horns, the rhythm of tyres on the road and Doppler effects ('sound poetry', co-founder Ralf Hütter dubbed it); vocals treated with a vocoder, percussion generated by electronic pads, phased synthesizer chords. Other artists, such as Yes or Tangerine Dream, had been using synths for longer, but strictly within prog-rock territory; Kraftwerk were the first to fully explore their possibilities within pop.

The closing section features the propulsive 'motorik' beat closely identified with peers Neu! and Can. Repetitive but evoking a propulsive momentum, it conveys the thrill of mechanized forward motion that became a recurring motif in Kraftwerk's oeuvre (see also 'Trans-Europe Express' and 'Tour de France').

State-of-the art technology enabled them to iron out human error: sequencers linked their drum machines to synthesizers, generating pristine rhythmic patterns ad infinitum – this at a time when many music critics and fans didn't accept the synth as an 'authentic' instrument. It seemed entirely fitting that BBC TV's science programme *Tomorrow's World* should showcase the group playing the song in September 1975.

'Autobahn' was new in a way that even Kraftwerk's genre-busting peers couldn't match: after all, you could trace Sex Pistols' roots back through the Stooges or MC5 to hard-edged Mod acts such as the Who. 'This may sound arrogant,' percussionist Wolfgang Flür told *Electronic Sound* in 2014, 'but rock sounded like something out of the Stone Age to us.' The single was to have a galvanizing impact on the electronica genre. To Mute Records' owner Daniel Miller, it was a revelation that 'electronic music could be poppy as well as being spacey and cosmic,' as he explained to *Electronic Sound*. Andy McCluskey, later of Orchestral Manoeuvres in the Dark, marvelled that Kraftwerk used electronic equipment to emulate real-world sounds. Or as Hütter put it: 'The noises from cars, coffee machines and vacuum cleaners, we can use for our music.'

Its parent album was a concept piece, setting a precedent for future Kraftwerk releases. The original German album featured a painted autobahn

Kraftwerk's definitive line-up (Karl Bartos, Ralf Hütter, Florian Schneider, Wolfgang Flür) look ahead

that effectively mirrored the retro-futurist feel of the music within. But the UK version was far more radical: a blue-and-white motorway sign, which the group adopted for later reissues, evidence that they were honing a singular aesthetic. Among those who took inspiration from its graphic minimalism was future Factory Records designer Peter Saville.

In 2019, Hütter described 'Autobahn' as a way of the band defining themselves as modern Germans. That meant swerving Anglo-American rock tropes and their country's post-war conservatism ('German society in the late 60s and 70s was still filled with figures from the Nazi era,' Neu!'s Michael Rother told *MOJO* in 2009). Instead, they looked to early 20th-century avant-garde movements such as Futurism and the Bauhaus, as well as ground-breaking *elektronische Musik* produced by pioneers such as Karlheinz Stockhausen.

Many music journalists lazily played on that post-war legacy when writing about German artists. In 1976, *NME* titled a review of their gig at London's Roundhouse 'Krautwerk: This is what your fathers fought to save you from'. The previous year, *Creem*'s Lester Bangs couldn't resist asking Kraftwerk whether brain-implanted electrodes that could transmit thoughts to a loudspeaker might be 'the final solution to the music problem'. The group's response was to slyly subvert such stereotypes. Hütter impishly advised Bangs that the German mentality 'is more advanced'. And Kraftwerk's look? Short haircuts, suits and ties – robot-like German efficiency? 'We knew our appearance was ironic, flirtatious, provocative,' Flür told *Uncut* in 2019. Music, artwork, presentation, ideology: one coherent concept.

With the band's 1977's *Trans-Europe Express*, everyone from Bronx hip-hoppers to Mancunian post-punk artists picked up on Kraftwerk. It all started with 'Autobahn', though.

'ELECTRONIC MUSIC IS A VERY LIQUID SITUATION, NOT LIKE ROCK'N'ROLL, WHICH IS A VERY STABLE FORMAT.'

RALF HÜTTER

South Bronx Soulsonic boy Afrika Bambaataa

Afrika Bambaataa and producer Arthur Baker sampled Kraftwerk's track 'Trans-Europe Express' (much favoured at South Bronx block parties) and 'Numbers' for 1982's electro-defining 'Planet Rock'. 'Trans-Europe Express' in particular became a building block for the electro scenes in New York and on the West Coast. 'What's the story of the birth of house music?' Phil Hartnoll mused to *Uncut* in 2004. 'US DJs mixing Kraftwerk with something else, isn't it?'

Detroit's techno music had Kraftwerk in its DNA, Derrick May famously describing it as 'like George Clinton and Kraftwerk stuck in an elevator with nothing but a sequencer to keep them occupied'. Among countless examples, Juan Atkins referenced 'Computer World' in 'Industrial Lies', while Carl Craig's *Landcruising* (1995) paid explicit homage to 'Autobahn'.

The effect Kraftwerk and their German peers had on David Bowie's career is well documented. Joy Division were devotees too and the wave of British synthesizer artists in the early 80s (Gary Numan, Depeche Mode, the Human League) openly acknowledged their debt to the Düsseldorf quartet.

From *Trans-Europe Express* onwards, Kraftwerk shared an identical look and assimilated a robotic motif into their aesthetic. This added mystique but also offered the deeply private Hütter and his cohort sanctuary from the media. Daft Punk, Deadmau5 and others learned those lessons well, while the 'motorik' beats would inform a vein of mechanically textured disco, notably Donna Summer's 'I Feel Love' (see p.124).

POETRY AND THE DAWN OF PUNK

HORSES
PATTI SMITH
1975

It starts with the sleeve, a monochrome portrait of a skinny girl-boy, shaggy black hair, staring us down, jacket louchely slung over a shoulder. Taken by Smith's then lover Robert Mapplethorpe, the photograph coolly explodes conventions of female beauty. The music within pairs blazing poetry with dynamic and supple musical support, from wisp-light to whirling roar. Art as rock'n'roll.

Horses kicks off with what remains Smith's most iconoclastic statement: a slow-burn reworking of Van Morrison's 'Gloria'. Its opening lines now rejected Christ Himself and His suffering for us, though Smith staunchly stuck to the original gender in the lyric, resulting in an openly lesbian love (lust?) letter.

The Sex Pistols and the Clash trashed the 1960s; Smith frankly cherished its firebrands. Her stunning overhaul of Jimi Hendrix's 'Hey Joe', into which she salaciously smuggles heiress-cum-terrorist Patty Hearst, was the A-side of her debut single 'Piss Factory'. Her core passion – poetry, especially that of unfettered souls such as Blake, Rimbaud, Baudelaire and the Beat Poets (Allen Ginsberg was a close friend) – further distinguishes *Horses* from the pack, and her impressionistic lyrics frequently expand into a stream-of-consciousness flow. Smith's voice pins you: sneering, coquettish, vulnerable, animalistic; never pretty. And death ('Redondo Beach', 'Land', 'Elegie', 'Birdland') is never far away.

Lead guitarist Lenny Kaye had assembled 1972's *Nuggets* compilation – a collection of snotty 60s psych garage bands that fed directly into punk, and Smith's group cut their teeth at New York punk haven CBGBs, alongside the likes of the Ramones. But unlike the latter's signature short, sharp musical shocks, *Horses* is a more nuanced prospect. As with Smith's contemporaries Television, multifaceted long-form works represent some of this album's highlights: both 'Birdland' and 'Land' are a Doors-ian nine minutes long. Her band provides tight but light-footed support: hushed piano trills open 'Break it Up' and 'Free Money', before chuntering rhythms take over; in 'Birdland', shards of guitar noise fleck Smith's incantatory declamations.

Even without the help of a lead single, or airplay, *Horses* broke the *Billboard* Top 50, an extraordinary feat for such a genre-bending underground album. A declamatory statement of intent and talent, *Horses* affirmed Smith's stature as a fiercely individualistic performer, and an inspiration to strong-minded female artists from contemporaries such as Viv Albertine of the Slits to Madonna, Courtney Love and Savages.

Smith in 1974, sporting a favourite rebel T-shirt

REVOLUTION FROM STUDIO TO STREET 1967–1976

THE PISTOLS' CALLING CARD

'ANARCHY IN THE UK'
SEX PISTOLS
1976

The Damned's 'New Rose' may have pipped it as the first British punk single, but that wasn't a hit. 'Anarchy in the UK' broke the Top 40 and was a far more dangerous proposition.

For a start, it was political – namedropping the IRA, UDA and Angola's MPLA, and intimating that violent civil unrest might be in the air for the UK too. Not unlikely: mid-70s Britain had seen strikes, power cuts, inflation spikes, three-day weeks and the rise of the National Front. Johnny Rotten sounds like chaos incarnate – as in Shelley's *Mask of Anarchy*: 'I am God, and King and Law!' – although in 2012, he complained to *MOJO*, '"Anarchy" for me was just the beginning of a debate... Nobody wanted to discuss what the song was really about.'

In spirit, it also called time on the music that had long dominated the charts and radio: indulgent progressive-rock groups, 60s hangovers, soft balladry – all too comfortable for those unstable, edgy days. Steve Jones's guitars are a brutal wall of sound, a rising wail of feedback escalating tension in the final verse. But not everyone was impressed: *NME* dismissed the single as 'laughably naïve... a third-rate Who imitation'.

Housed in a shiny black sleeve, 'Anarchy in the UK' was released by EMI on 26 November 1976. But elements within EMI were already unhappy about the Pistols' attendant controversy: workers at their Hayes factory refused to bag the single; distribution hit snags. Five days later, the group were a last-minute stand-in for Queen on Thames Television's *The Today Show*. Rotten and Jones (particularly Jones) swore live on air. Now the single was banned and withdrawn (it stalled at No.38). On 6 January 1977, EMI officially dropped the Pistols. In smart succession, local councils began cancelling dates on the band's forthcoming UK tour.

Then again, the Pistols had been setting off mini musical earthquakes for months. Urged on by Howard Devoto and Pete Shelley of Buzzcocks, they played Manchester's Lesser Free Trade Hall on 4 June (entry: 50p), returning six weeks later. The crowds were sparse on both nights, but included future members of Joy Division, Buzzcocks, Mark E. Smith of the Fall and Morrissey of the Smiths. 'Everything that happens is still a fall-out of the Sex Pistols coming to the Lesser Free Trade Hall,' music writer Paul Morley (who was at the first gig) stated years later. 'There's no doubt about it. You can draw it all back to that little explosion.'

Rotten at Queensway Hall, Dunstable, in October 1976, the month before 'Anarchy' descended on the UK

REVOLUTION FROM STUDIO TO STREET 1967–1976

PUNK TO POST-PUNK

You can find traces of punk in 60s garage bands such as the Sonics, the Rolling Stones' belligerency or the Who's early singles and onstage destruction. Detroit's MC5 played primal rock'n'roll and were explosive onstage, while the glammed-up New York Dolls tapped into rock'n'roll's first flush. Punk simmers across the Stooges' splenetic debut, while Sex Pistol Steve Jones claimed he learned guitar by playing along to their 1973 set *Raw Power* on speed.

The Pistols were a catalyst for the British punk explosion, a big bang from which a new musical universe rushed forth. The Damned's haywire energy and speed-of-light songs. The Clash: raw-throated social protest with a political edge. Manchester's Buzzcocks: witty chroniclers of teenage angst whose 'Spiral Scratch' EP proved doubly influential – as an inspirational self-funded release and a shot across the bows of the London-centric music industry.

By its very nature, punk had an inbuilt sell-by date. In its wake, artists such as Blondie, Elvis Costello, or the Pretenders paired its energy to pop nous in what became new wave. Others broadened its palette, taking in reggae and dub, electronica, jazz and avant-garde sound creation, while retaining its bite, giving rise to the loose agglomeration 'post-punk'. Punk's 'year zero' ethos slammed the door on swathes of past music; post-punk opened it again.

By 1978, Johnny Rotten had reverted to his birth name John Lydon and assembled Public Image Limited (PiL), with whom he tracked more nebulous aspects of the human condition – notably on 1979's *Metal Box*. Siouxsie and the Banshees evolved a churning, hypnotic quality to their sound, driven by intricate powerhouse drums. On *London Calling*, the Clash expanded their core punk sound to incorporate rockabilly, reggae, ska and pop.

Punk's thrashed power chords gave way to spiky, angular textures and scratchiness (see Gang of Four's 'Damaged Goods'), metallic sheets of sound (PiL's Keith Levene) or polymorphous musicianship (John McGeoch of Magazine and the Banshees). Television played punk haven CBGBs alongside the Ramones,

Joy Division take it to the bridge. Hulme, Manchester, 1979

but their exploratory guitar lines and abstruse lyrics made them an artier prospect. Rhythms became jerkier, less predictable (see Devo's 'Jocko Homo' or their cover of the Rolling Stones' 'Satisfaction').

Part of post-punk's strength was that it drew on a rich reservoir of non-musical influences. Punk band Warsaw became Joy Division, whose lead singer Ian Curtis penned troubled lyrics informed by his admiration for the sci-fi dystopias of J.G. Ballard and Franz Kafka's nightmarish scenarios. The Fall's sound evolved regularly, not least because of the high turnover of its members, but lyricist/singer Mark E. Smith (whose inspirations ranged from Friedrich Nietzsche to Philip K. Dick) was an abrasive constant. The similarly literate Morrissey's lyrics of perennial outsiderdom, coupled with Johnny Marr's ecstatic and inventive guitar playing, would make the Smiths Britain's most important band in the early 1980s. All three game-changers, all three from Manchester.

By the mid 1980s, post-punk had diversified into an abundance of genres, ranging from goth to neo-psychedelia and indie shoegazing. Few artists shape-shifted like Joy Division, though. Reborn as New Order in the wake of Ian Curtis's suicide, they embraced dance music and worked with Arthur Baker to create 'Blue Monday', the bestselling 12-inch single of all time.

BEATS AND THE BEATEN GENERATION

1977–1999

In 1977, the year of Elizabeth II's Silver Jubilee, Sex Pistols' savage 'God Save the Queen' aroused widespread disgust and ill-feeling. Singer Johnny Rotten (whom one tabloid dubbed 'the biggest threat to our youth since Hitler') was attacked with a razor, drummer Paul Cook assailed with an iron bar.

As British prime minister from 1979, Margaret Thatcher oversaw a period of economic growth but also growing inequalities. At the dawn of the 1980s, aggressive police stop-and-search powers – disproportionately affecting people of colour and ethnic minorities – and a major recession with unemployment topping three million led to unrest and violence in city centres, which also played out in the era's music. The Specials' bleak 'Ghost Town' hit No.1 in July 1981 as riots flared in around 20 cities and towns, while the previous year fellow ska aficionados the Beat had begged 'Stand Down, Margaret'.

Initially unpopular, Thatcher's stock rose following Britain's victory in the Falklands War with Argentina, and by the middle of the decade, rising wages and a boom in house prices and stock markets ushered in the 'Yuppie' era. A period of conspicuous consumption came to define the 80s – something reflected in the exotic imagery and lifestyles depicted in videos by New Romantic artists such as Duran Duran. In the USA, Republican President Ronald Reagan – a natural political bedfellow for the right-wing Thatcher – presided over a parallel economic upswing, along with an escalation in the arms race with the Soviet Union (which Reagan dubbed an 'evil empire'). By the end of the decade, and the fall of the Berlin Wall, that empire had dissolved.

In the mid 1980s, while British pop succumbed to Stock, Aitken and Waterman's glossy, identikit pop productions, a radical new strain of dance music reasserted itself in the form of acid house. Just as rock and rap had crossed over earlier in the decade, dancefloor beats began infiltrating guitar pop, notably in British indie-dance artists such as Primal Scream. Their *Screamadelica* (1991) set – significantly shaped by producers Andrew Weatherall and Hugo Nicolson – helped define the era, along with Manchester bands such as the Stone Roses and Happy Mondays, whose loose-fitting clothes (better for dancing) inspired the 'baggy' moniker.

Stateside rock diversified wildly. Bad boys Guns N' Roses became metal's Big New Thing, with their *Appetite for Destruction* album smoothing their rise to stadium status; Red Hot Chili Peppers got there by seasoning their rock with funk. Grunge offered a dressed-down punk-metal mash-up, with Seattle acts such as Nirvana and Mudhoney in the vanguard, while riot grrrl acts such as Bikini Kill paired underground punk to a feminist ethos. Meanwhile, Metallica's eponymous fifth set, known as 'the Black Album' (1991), would enjoy 16x platinum sales, driven by classics such as 'Enter Sandman', turning them from cult artists to globe-straddling rock stars and sending metal into the mainstream.

At the same time, so-called Britpop arose in the UK, a loose conglomeration of retro-friendly acts embracing artier outfits such as Suede, Blur and Pulp, and post-punk-inflected Elastica. The Beatles-indebted Oasis outsold the lot of them, but pop quintet Spice Girls trounced everyone, becoming a worldwide pop phenomenon with their take on 'Girl Power'. Mainstream pop had a new queen in Britney Spears, while a boy-band trend embraced Backstreet Boys, *NSYNC and Britain's Take That.

In the States, R&B had a new lease of life with the likes of Janet Jackson and Mary J. Blige, while Lauryn Hill and TLC expanded the genre with hip-hop sensibilities. Three ex-NWA stars – Ice Cube, Eazy-E and Dr Dre – helped define the controversial guns-n-girls-toting Gangsta Rap. It was Dre who set the template for G-Funk with his set *The Chronic* (1992), and a year later produced Snoop Dogg's *Doggystyle*, which became the first debut album by an artist to debut at No.1 on *Billboard*.

In 1992, after four LA cops submitted black suspect Rodney King to a prolonged and violent beating (secretly captured on videotape by an onlooker), riots flared up across the city in a grim echo of late 1960s urban conflagrations. Gangsta rap's emergence was a reflection of the turbulent times, as rivalry between East and West Coast artists and labels spilled over into provocative taunts in songs and (in the case of Tupac Shakur and the Notorious BIG) murder.

'I DON'T HAVE THE ANSWERS FOR ANYTHING. I DON'T WANT TO BE A F*****G SPOKESPERSON.'

KURT COBAIN

1977

→ Sex Pistols release 'God Save the Queen'.

→ Celebrated disco club Studio 54 opens in Manhattan.

→ Fela Kuti's 1976 *Zombie* album openly criticizes the government and military in Nigeria. Partly in response, his home compound is destroyed in a violent raid.

→ Release of *Star Wars* (later retitled *Episode IV: A New Hope*).

1978

→ Birth of the world's first 'test tube baby', Louise Joy Brown, via in vitro fertilization (IVF).

1979

→ An Islamic revolution overthrows the Shah of Iran. Ayatollah Khomeini replaces him as head of state.

→ 'Rapper's Delight' by the Sugarhill Gang becomes the first major rap hit, reaching no.36 on *Billboard*.

→ Margaret Thatcher becomes the UK's first female prime minister.

1980

→ John Lennon is shot dead by a deranged fan outside his New York home, the Dakota Building.

→ Seagate pioneer the first computer hard-disk drive.

1981

→ Ronald Reagan becomes the 40th US president.

1982

→ Michael Jackson's *Thriller* released, accompanied by a game-changing video for the title track.

→ Release of 'The Message', one of hip-hop's earliest socially aware tracks, credited to Grandmaster Flash and the Furious Five.

→ Ridley Scott's *Blade Runner* premieres.

→ The first CDs go on sale.

1983

→ MIDI technology is born.

→ New Order's 'Blue Monday' is released. It will go on to become the bestselling 12-inch single of all time.

1985

→ Discovery of a hole in the ozone layer over Antarctica.

1986
→ The first African Nobel laureate is crowned: writer Wole Soyinka.

1988
→ Acid house raves start up in empty warehouses across the UK as the 'Second Summer of Love' arrives.

1989
→ The Berlin Wall is taken down.
→ The Soviet Union withdraws from Afghanistan.

1990
→ Saddam Hussein's Iraqi forces invade Kuwait, prompting the first Gulf War the following year.
→ Tim Berners-Lee demonstrates the World Wide Web and the HyperText Markup Language (HTML).

1991
→ Dissolution of the USSR.
→ Release of Nirvana's *Nevermind* album.
→ India's prime minister Rajiv Gandhi is assassinated.
→ Metallica's landmark fifth album (known as 'The Black Album') is released. It will go on to sell some 16 million-plus copies in the USA alone.

1992
→ The Maastricht Treaty inaugurates the European Union.
→ Premiere of Quentin Tarantino's *Reservoir Dogs*.

1994
→ Jeff Bezos founds Amazon, initially as an online bookstore.
→ Nelson Mandela becomes South Africa's first Black president.

1996
→ Dolly the Sheep becomes the first mammal cloned from an adult cell.

1997
→ *Sensation* exhibition of Young British Artists debuts at London's Royal Academy of Arts.
→ J.K. Rowling's *Harry Potter and the Philosopher's Stone* is published.

1998
→ Larry Page and Sergey Brin launch Google.

THE FUTURE OF DANCE MUSIC

'I FEEL LOVE'
DONNA SUMMER
1977

With *I Remember Yesterday*, Summer, along with producers Giorgio Moroder and Pete Bellotte, had planned an album covering pop music across time, from 40s swing to whatever the future might hold. For the final track, they came up with what they thought might sound like space-age disco. It put the rest of the album firmly in the shade.

'I Feel Love' proved that electronic music didn't have to be cold; here, it's sensual, erotic, ecstatic, sexy – and supremely danceable in a way that Kraftwerk's sleek 'Trans-Europe Express' and 'Europe Endless' (released the same year) weren't, but which shares their hypnotic ambience. Synthesized rhythms and tones replaced the sweet string sections that had studded so many disco tunes. A juddering bass line – on a borrowed Moog Modular 3P synth – complemented the throbbing electro pulse. The Moog periodically went out of tune, so Moroder and Bellotte had to patiently piece together the bass part from short snippets.

The track was an entirely in-the-box electronic creation save for Summer's cooed, delirious vocals and a bass drum. By accident, an engineer put a delay on the beat that happened to be at the same tempo, effectively doubling the song's pulse, making it more insistent – one reason why 'I Feel Love' became part of the DNA of electro disco, Hi-NRG, house and techno. Remarkably, a remix the following year by Patrick Cowley is almost as noteworthy, extending the ecstasy to around the 15-minute mark while retaining the original's mesmerizing pull.

'I Feel Love' was a UK No.1 (for four weeks), and a No.6 and a gay dance staple Stateside, but stood apart from its disco peers. Rather like the Sugarhill Gang's 'Rapper's Delight', what might have been a novelty (like 1972's synth-led hit 'Popcorn', say, or Space's electronically nuanced 'Magic Fly', a hit in the summer of 1977) became a stepping stone to an entirely new sound world.

Brian Eno knew it immediately. Then in the midst of working with David Bowie on a trio of game-changing albums in Berlin, he told the singer, 'This is it, look no further. This single is going to change the sound of club music for the next 15 years.' And counting.

Prima Donna: Summer in fine feather, late 1970s

BEATS AND THE BEATEN GENERATION 1977–1999

ALL-FEMALE, REGGAE-DRIVEN POST-PUNK ENVELOPE-PUSHER

CUT
THE SLITS
1979

They'd played on the Clash's *White Riot* tour, but were regularly pilloried for their gleefully ramshackle sets. And because they were women, even some punks didn't take them seriously. *Cut* feels like sweet revenge.

However much reggae they might have listened to in their downtime, punk's frontline acts – the Clash aside – mostly avoided it on record and live, instead playing hell-for-leather upstart rock music. The Slits, as in so many other respects, were an exception. Pivotal punk scenester Don Letts – briefly their manager – had played dub reggae during his DJ stints at the Roxy, and its rhythms cross-cut this album's sound.

In contrast to punk's all-guns-blazing ramalam, *Cut* is all about space, allowing instruments to breathe, backing vocals bouncing off and interweaving with the lead voice. Guitarist Viv Albertine felt reggae went hand in glove with the Slits' aesthetic: 'Dub seemed to have a femininity about it; it was more fluid.' Producer Dennis Bovell had a foot in both dub and sweet lovers rock pop (he'd produced Janet Kay's 'Silly Games'), making him an ideal foil for a group that paired untutored exuberance and risk-taking with a gift for hooks and melody. In 2009, bassist Tessa Pollitt described their style to *The Quietus* as 'Instinctive female music. We weren't trying to play like men.'

'Typical Girls' – a near hit – was a manifesto, skewering conventional expectations about how women should behave and appear. In 2015, guitarist Viv Albertine affirmed: 'We were on a mission, not just to show that women had a place in music but to show alternatives in how to act and dress, speak, walk.' Few A-list punk artists had wit to match their bite (honourable exceptions include Buzzcocks and John Cooper Clarke) as the Slits do here. The track isn't just a satire on stereotypes, but a proper pop song too.

The single's B-side – their extraordinary deconstruction of the Motown classic 'Heard it Through the Grapevine' – rivals it as their greatest achievement, Ari Up's vocal a force unto itself, and Max 'Maxi' Edwards' crisp beats is an anchor for the group's energy. (For *Cut*, Budgie – soon to become drummer for Siouxsie's Banshees – took over, his playing busily inventive but always to the point.)

For all their ground-breaking music and attitude, the Slits were actually very young women – Ari Up just 17. Hence, 'Ping Pong Affair' recounts the disappointments of below-par boyfriends and 'Love und Romance' satirizes romantic clichés, while elsewhere they merrily recount the pleasures of

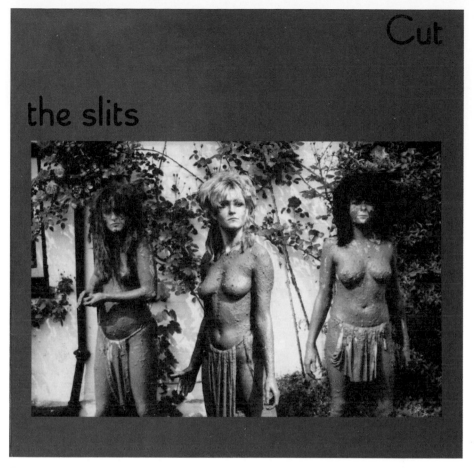

Muddy daughters

'Shoplifting'. Meanwhile, 'So Tough' satirizes the patronizing attitudes the Slits faced even among their punk peers.

At the time, all the Slits were enamoured of one particular Dionne Warwick compilation featuring mostly Burt Bacharach and Hal David songs; Albertine and Ari Up studied its polished popcraft and arrangements, warping them into their own off-kilter, utterly original writing. In her 2014 memoir *Clothes, Clothes, Clothes, Music, Music, Music, Boys, Boys, Boys*, Albertine revealed that the anonymous guitar player on the album (who played mostly on the offbeat, reggae style) fed into her own technique – here jagged, scratchy, economical. Most male rock guitarists she found too egotistical and flashy, too indebted to twelve-bar-blues traditions. 'We had no heroes,' Ari Up insisted to *The Quietus* in 2009. 'We had no one to look up to... I didn't use Patti Smith as my big hero.'

The cover was a controversy in itself: three defiantly bare-breasted Slits clad only in loincloths and mud. Some stores refused to stock the album, *Melody Maker*'s editor found it distasteful, and even though *NME* put the muddy trio on its cover, it couldn't help riffing on the *Sun*'s Page Three Girls for its headline. 'It was quite menacing, like warrior women,' reflected bassist Tessa Pollitt in Zoë Street Howe's 2009 biography *Typical Girls*. 'A powerful cover whether you like it or not.'

Contemporaries such as the Raincoats (featuring ex-Slits drummer Palmolive) and the Pop Group clearly absorbed, and learned from, *Cut*, though both the album and the band's untempered, in-your-face attitude had more far-reaching impact, from later punk musicians such as Kim Gordon through to the riot grrrl movement.

'WE WERE TRYING TO WRITE GREAT POP SONGS, BUT ENDED UP CREATING SOMETHING NEW BY ACCIDENT.'

VIV ALBERTINE

Female artists all too often ran up against the same prejudices within the punk movement as in the greater world. Which adds extra bite to the work of singular artists such as Poly Styrene of X-Ray Spex, writer of vibrant salvos savaging materialistic society: 'Oh Bondage Up Yours!', 'Art-I-Ficial' and 'Identity'. But also 'Germ Free Adolescents', a satire on obsessive cleanliness in a perfect pop tune. And her look – multiracial, dental braces, throwback 60s jackets and handbags – made her one of punk's truest don't-give-a-damn icons.

Siouxsie and the Banshees swiftly outgrew punk's trappings, aided by the astonishing drumming of Budgie and featuring one of the period's most distinctive guitarists in John McGeoch. Sioux herself became an icon both for her distinctive look – part 1920s flapper, part vampiress, part *Snow White*'s Evil Queen – and declamatory vocals. Alongside inspirational artists such as Nick Cave, she's frequently cited as a major influence on goth, though from 'Spellbound' through 'Christine' to her genre-hopping releases with then partner Budgie as the Creatures, her work defies easy categorization.

Patti Smith's free-wheeling, confrontational verse and non-conformist stance was set in a tradition of rebellious mavericks from William Blake and Arthur Rimbaud to Bob Dylan and Keith Richards. But alongside the androgynous Smith, punk had its own Marilyn Monroe in Blondie's Debbie Harry, someone who hung with the Ramones and Iggy Pop and (with paramour Chris Stein) wrote killer, sharp-edged pop songs, while looking *Vogue*-chic.

The Raincoats' maintained a lower profile, but their lo-fi noise rock would have an enduring influence on non-conformist indie guitar bands in the 1980s and beyond (witness Kurt Cobain's fervent tribute to them in his liner notes for the 1992 Nirvana compilation *Insesticide*).

A LANDMARK RELEASE
FOR SAMPLING

MY LIFE IN THE BUSH OF GHOSTS
BRIAN ENO AND DAVID BYRNE
1981

By the start of the 1980s, the incorporation of found sound into music was a widely acknowledged compositional technique, though still at the margins of popular culture. Brian Eno was a long-time admirer of maverick composer and thinker John Cage, and sometimes referred to himself as a non-musician, so it made perfect sense that he should bring an out-of-the-box approach to the album he was planning with Talking Heads frontman, David Byrne.

Stationed in California at the start of 1980, Eno and Byrne became fascinated by the evangelical preachers they heard on the radio – the mesmerizing rhythms and borderline frenzy of their delivery. Always with an eye to moving on, Eno had become attracted to the notion of incorporating 'found' vocals rather than singing himself, whether from the radio or recordings. He'd experienced that process first-hand while sitting on sessions for the 1979 album *Movies*, by ex-Can bassist Holger Czukay – so-called not only because Czukay sampled from movies, but because his composition process was comparable to film editing. Byrne's musical input included the distinctively jerky funk lines that he'd honed with Talking Heads, and contributions to the album's singular percussion, including a frying pan and biscuit tin.

Alongside radio broadcasts, there are samples from little-known ethnic-music albums – notably *Music in the World of Islam Vol.1 (Human Voices/Lutes)* and a set by the Moving Star Hall Singers gospel group from the Georgia Sea Islands, who sang in a beguiling local Creole. There are even the harsh caws of a parliament of rooks, recorded live by the owner of a stately home in Northumberland where Eno stayed in the summer of 1980. Under these play insistent rhythms, with limited chord changes, an approach Eno had absorbed from his adored Fela Kuti albums.

The effect is not unlike Marshall McLuhan's 'global village', as might be glimpsed by turning a radio tuner across bandwidths. To *Sounds* in 1981, Eno described it as his 'African psychedelic vision', but at one point the pair discussed using the concept of creating music from a fictitious foreign culture, and something of that vision survives. The album certainly offered something of an insight into world music – then literally a new world to many Western ears – but wasn't unconditionally welcomed. 'Jezebel Spirit' samples the unsettling sound of an anonymous exorcist in full flow on the radio; *Rolling Stone*'s Jon Pareles thought its appropriation belittled the event. And to avoid offending

The thinking person's pop stars

Muslim listeners, the track 'Qu'ran' – incorporating chants from the sacred book by Algerian worshippers – was deleted from later copies.

There's no doubting the album's musical impact, though. On the website created for the 2006 reissue, Hank Shocklee, of Public Enemy's production combo the Bomb Squad, recalled that it 'opened my head up to new musical and most importantly non-musical experiences'.

INDUSTRIAL NOISE MILESTONE

KOLLAPS
EINSTÜRZENDE NEUBAUTEN
1981

In the year that Stravinsky's *The Rite of Spring* sent Paris aquiver, Futurist Luigi Russolo penned *The Art of Noises*, praising noise as the next progression in music's evolution. To that end, Russolo made his own *intonarumori* – 'noise machines' – and composed works with titles such as *The Meeting of Automobiles and Aeroplanes*. Within a decade, composers including Eric Satie and George Antheil had incorporated typewriters, sirens and a (blank-firing) pistol into their compositions.

With *Kollaps*, Einstürzende Neubauten took on that same avant-garde zeal. The group chose not to use a traditional drum kit, forcing them to utilize found objects (mostly metal) for percussion instead. They were a trio, two of whom – N.U. Unruh and F.M. Einheit – were percussionists, with guitarist Blixa Bargeld filling in on everything else. Importantly, the group used contact microphones attached directly to the metal being struck, which picked up the range of vibrations within the object.

Incorporating saws, hammers, drills, metal plates and a catalogue of terrifying declamations from Bargeld – all improvised, sometimes distorted – it makes for joltingly uneasy listening. Little wonder the band's website describes the album as a declaration of war on 'all conventional listening habits'.

This is intensely claustrophobic music, purveying nihilism and apocalypse (hence the album title). On opener 'Tanz Debil' ('Dance Retardedly'), guitars saw against relentless drums. 'Sehnsucht' ('Addiction') nags like a migraine. 'Negativ Nein' ('Negative No') goes from sinister pattering to unhinged screams. 'Abstieg & Zerfall' ('Descent & Decay') evokes an ambience of dread, guitars buzzing like angry insects. Another title advises 'Hören mit Schmerzen' ('Listen with Pain'). The beat on the eight-minute title track was, Bargeld told the *Esoterica* podcast in May 2021, 'the most totalitarian kind of rhythm possible'; it also marked the debut of Neubauten's amplified metal spring, standing in for a bass drum. Implausibly, there's even a disjointed cover ('Jet'm') of Serge Gainsbourg and Jane Birkin's 'Je T'aime... Moi Non Plus', a screeching organ briefly interrupted by a wild vocal flurry. Even the quieter passages evoke tension, for – rather like watching a horror movie – who knows what's around the corner?

Such is the violent energy discharged on each song, however, that the album feels almost cathartic. Shocking, disorientating, but also a radical shake-up of what we describe as music.

Uneasy listening: the young Neubauten

'ONE OF THE MOST SHOCKING VISIONS EVER COMMITTED TO VINYL.'

TROUSER PRESS MAGAZINE

THE ROSETTA STONE
OF TURNTABLISM

'THE ADVENTURES OF GRANDMASTER FLASH ON THE WHEELS OF STEEL'
GRANDMASTER FLASH
1981

In the early 1970s, Bronx DJ Clive 'Kool Herc' Campbell had begun using
two turntables, each playing the same record, to extend a track's percussive
section (creating 'break beats') during parties. At a bash for his sister in
1973, he provided the backing for a friend – Coke La Rock – to rhyme over
(competitive wordplay – not infrequently boastful or socially weighted –
and Jamaican 'toasting' were well established in African-American musical
tradition; Herc himself came from Jamaica). In tandem, fellow New Yorker
Grand Wizzard Theodore was pioneering 'scratching' – moving the vinyl under
the deck's needle to create a percussive sound or rhythm (his signature was
'a nice clean scratch that didn't sound distorted,' he explained to DJHistory.com
in 1998). Herc and Afrika Bambaataa are recognized as two of hip-hop's holy
trinity. But the third member of the trio, Joseph 'Grandmaster Flash' Saddler,
took turntablism to another level.

　　Released on the Sugar Hill label as a 12-inch single, 'The Adventures of
Grandmaster Flash on the Wheels of Steel' was the first track to be created
entirely from samples. Its core components are Chic's 'Good Times', Queen's
Chic-influenced 'Another One Bites the Dust', Spoonie Gee's 'Monster Jam'
and Blondie's 'Rapture' – the 1980 single that became rap's first US No.1 and
which referenced Flash alongside Fab 5 Freddy at a time when precious few
people outside the Bronx had heard of either. Perhaps there was a sly irony at
work here, in blending Queen's track with the Chic track that so heavily inspired
it. (The track's title nods to mid-60s LP *The Official Adventures of Flash Gordon*,
which Flash scavenges for spoken-word inserts.) The single was true to the kind
of hip-hop then being heard in the South Bronx – unlike the Sugarhill Gang's
lighter, disco-friendly fare.

　　It was a found-sound fantasy: none of the music was original, but Flash's
treatment of it was – outrageously so. The song doesn't have a chorus. And he
didn't create it using tape edits, as disco remix pioneers such as Tom Moulton
had (see p.90); Flash performed the complex mix entirely live, alternating
between *three* decks and cueing up the records by adding notes to their labels.
'Good Times' is the anchor, the root the listener can return to for reassurance,
around which snatches of the other songs (which also include 'The Birthday
Party' and 'Freedom', both featuring rappers the Furious Five, with whom Flash's
name became synonymous) assume the role of a verse or instrumental break.

Flash captains the wheels in the early 80s

BEATS AND THE BEATEN GENERATION 1977–1999

At a stroke, Flash demonstrated the creative potential of using snippets from pre-existing recordings to construct a new track – cheap and hugely effective, albeit singularly unprofitable for the original artists. His cutting and scratching set new benchmarks for hip-hop in his use of backspin on discs and 'juggling' beats from two copies of the same record to generate a new beat.

Aside from those dextrous deck skills, he helped pioneer other techniques that became essential parts of a hip-hop DJ's arsenal, such as using headphones to cue up the percussion breaks in a record so that, along with a self-built cross-fader system (effectively, a mixer), he could monitor the mix, switch between channels and seamlessly dovetail beats from two separate records. (Previously, a DJ would locate them on sight: thick grooves on vinyl meant the drum break.) Ditto his discovery that spray-starching and then ironing the two sides of a felt disc created a slipmat.

Its impact on one of hip-hop's future sonic visionaries was immediate and absolute: 'I immediately went home and called some friends and we were taking apart one of my friend's mother's stereo sets,' Andre 'Dr Dre' Young told *Vibe* magazine in 2010. 'We figured out how to make a mixer from the balance button and got it cracking – started making mixtapes.'

Hip-hop's potential for social commentary came to blazing fruition on 1982's bleak 'The Message' (a UK No.8) – credited to both Flash and the Furious Five, although his involvement was minimal. But his single-handed tour de force 'The Adventures of Grandmaster Flash on the Wheels of Steel' was a revolution in its own right.

'IT MADE ME WANT TO KNOW WHAT HIP-HOP WAS. THAT WAS THE SONG THAT DID IT.'

DR DRE

Three is the magic number: De La Soul, 1991

In the early 1980s, new technology dramatically upped hip hop's game. Cheap, compact samplers such as Akai's MPC series (notably the MPC60) and E-MU SP-1200, along with drum machines such as Roland's TR808, enabled hip hop artists to create entire songs without stepping inside a recording studio. And with the debut of Akai's S900 in 1986, they could store and edit some 30 sound files simultaneously, and loop them.

'Crate-digging' for rare vinyl became an obsession. The era represented a pre-copyright Wild West, with the entire history of recorded music open to producers. Take three core 1989 releases: De La Soul's epochal *Three Feet High and Rising* contains 60 samples, the Beastie Boys' career-redefining *Paul's Boutique* has 100-plus and there are more than 20 on Public Enemy's incendiary 'Fight the Power'. To listeners wise to the original source, it opened up additional layers of meaning, sometimes implying respect or lineage.

The end came in 1991: following the *Grand Upright Music, Ltd v. Warner Bros. Records, Inc.* case, samples had to be cleared by the artist before use. With existing music now legally protected, artists made hard choices – Kendrick Lamar's *Damn.* (2017) has fewer than 20 samples. But samples in and of themselves were only ever a start: it's how they're used that marks out an artist's originality.

AFROPOP CROSSES OVER

JUJU MUSIC
KING SUNNY ADÉ AND HIS AFRICAN BEATS
1982

King Sunny Adé was a major musical force in his homeland of Nigeria by the time *Juju Music* appeared, a prolific recording artist averaging around four albums per year and the head of his own label. Like his famous compatriot Fela Kuti (see p.102), Adé was of the Yoruba people – Africa's largest tribe – but while Kuti remained at loggerheads with Nigeria's government, Adé swerved controversy and remained hugely popular. Kuti might rail and spit out his anger; Adé's delivery was unerringly sweet and calm. It was *Juju Music*, more than any other, that opened Western ears to Nigerian sounds.

A band incorporating around 20 musicians, plus additional vocalists, unleashes joyful, multilayered reworkings of seven of Adé's Nigerian hits, riding on interplay between a handful of guitars, steel guitar (which he introduced to juju) and call-and-response between drums and vocalists, but also mysterious dub-style interventions. And – of course – irresistible rhythms generated by a rich variety of percussion, including the West African Iya Ilu – the 'talking drum' that can be made to mimic the inflections of the human voice, and has long been juju music's predominant sound – but also a Linn drum machine. That dovetailing of old and new musical technologies is typical of the album: 'Mo Beru Agba' opens with talking-drum chatter and massed vocals, but then ethereal waves of synthesizer sound waft in.

In the year of its release, Adé and his group brought *Juju Music* (his major-label debut for Mango, the world music subsidiary of Chris Blackwell's Island Records) to Europe and the USA, where huge crowds lapped up the concerted tightness and complex arrangements of the band's grooves. In December, the *New York Times* hailed it as 'the year's freshest dance-music album', while *NME* rated it among the Top 10 albums of 1982. US critics hailed him as a Bob Marley in waiting, and although he never ascended to that throne (for one thing, unlike Marley, he sang in his native tongue, rather than English), *Juju Music* was pivotal in arousing an appetite and passion for Afropop in the West.

The King on tour in Chicago, Illinois, in 1983

BEATS AND THE BEATEN GENERATION 1977–1999

KATE BUSH LETS THE WEIRDNESS IN

THE DREAMING
KATE BUSH
1982

Kate Bush first used a Fairlight CMI synth/sampler on *Never For Ever* (1980), whose aural palette includes the sounds of cocked rifles ('Army Dreamers') and breaking glass ('Babooshka'). But it became her go-to tool for her fourth LP *The Dreaming*, on which she transformed herself from eccentric pop waif into trailblazing experimentalist.

The album was Bush's big leap into the dark, not only because it was angrier and riskier than previous releases, but also because she assumed the role of producer for the first time. Rather than compose at the piano, her usual approach, she focused on building up arresting rhythm patterns (three musicians are separately credited with playing sticks), and unfamiliar textures.

The expansive instrumentation included a didgeridoo, bouzouki, uilleann pipes and even a bullroarer. A string quartet provides interludes on 'Houdini' (on the album's cover Bush is his wife, Bess, secretly passing a key to her husband). Engineers Nick Launay and Paul Hardiman were veterans of albums by PiL and Wire respectively, shaping the album's wrong-footing twists and turns.

One creative constant is Bush's gift for constructing each song as a narrative in its own right, like a short story, though sometimes we arrive at the middle, and sometimes we never get to the end. The pounding 'Sat in Your Lap' (the sole hit single, a UK No.11) explores how a hunger for knowledge is so easily undermined by the lack of necessary effort. It reels on awkward accents and tribal beats, the vocals alternately cooing and off-her-head strident, vaulting suddenly skyward. Throughout the album, she's pushing her voice – into hoarse screams, full-throated declamations, masculine depths; assuming accents, doubling herself.

In 'Pull Out the Pin', a Vietcong soldier stalks an American GI by his scent. 'The Dreaming' itself references Aboriginal land being mined for minerals to make weapons, didgeridoo and animal calls (voiced by impressionist Percy Edwards) informing its ethnic ambience, set against the bang of Fairlight-generated car doors. In the nightmarish closer 'Get Out of My House' – punctuated by sampled door slams – bricks and mortar stand in for a hurt individual, locking out an ostensibly evil force (a violent ex-lover?) and defiantly braying in its face. But in this nuanced song, self-defence can be self-imprisonment too.

The Dreaming made the UK Top 3, but counfounded fans and critics alike. Its appetite for invention impacted on later mavericks, though, including Björk (it became her favourite Kate Bush album) and OutKast's Big Boi. Bush dubbed this extraordinary creative leap forward her 'she's gone mad' album. But who wants sane, safe art?

What Kate did next: Bush at Abbey Road's fabled Studio 2, London, 1982

BEATS AND THE BEATEN GENERATION 1977–1999

DIGITAL RECORDING AND THE CD

In 1979, the Fairlight CMI went on sale, one of the earliest digital audio workstations (DAW), digital synthesizers and samplers. It was to have a major impact on the way more innovative 'rock' artists worked – notably Peter Gabriel, who owned the first Series 1 Fairlight CMI in the UK, and Kate Bush.

The Fairlight became a core tool for hip-hop artists too. Afrika Bambaata, Arthur Baker and John Robie worked out a way of playing one sample – 'ORCH5', taken from part of a recording of Igor Stravinsky's *Firebird* suite – eight times simultaneously for 'Planet Rock'. Just one second long, the sample has been used multiple times since, by everyone from Yes to Bruno Mars.

Magnetic tape had revolutionized the possibilities for manipulating sound in the 1940s and 1950s. MIDI (Musical Instrument Digital Interface) did it again, starting in 1983. For the first time, hardware and computers could communicate with each other. That year's Steinberg's Cubase introduced an interface that persists to this day: the arrange page, in which individual tracks (arranged vertically on the left) run horizontally, left to right, for the duration of the music. Naturally, a musician could still input the sounds from instruments into the workspace of the song, but with the introduction of plug-ins in 1996 as part of Cubase VST, processing could take place within a MIDI software program. Three years later, Cubase VST 3.7 debuted plug-in instruments.

In time, MIDI would permit its user to view everything about a song from the arrangement and duration of its notes to their attack and volume on a computer screen. Appearing as blocks of sound, they could be cut up, looped, rearranged, reversed, drowned in a well of reverb – tinkered with ad infinitum. Out-of-sync drumbeats could be snapped back into perfect time by quantizing; pitch correction rectified wobbly vocals. With the 21st century, the choices of DAW software expanded to include Reason, Ableton Live, Logic and Pro Tools. And you could use a software program to master and mix your music to a sophisticated level too. Cost-effective (today, much of

Ryuichi Sakamoto, with a Fairlight CMI Series III sampling synth and a Yamaha DX7 keyboard, on stage in 1988

the technology is available online for free) and space-saving, music software facilitated the rise of the bedroom artist/producer.

Digital recording harboured aesthetic drawbacks too, though. Less talented, or lazy, practitioners would simply use an original sample wholesale. Then there's the danger that too many home-based musicians/producers wind up using the same in-the-box loops and effects. Partly to swerve that possibility, more innovative artists began seeking out original analogue hardware, such as MiniMoog synths, both for their period sonic fingerprints and to instil their work with organic textures.

Digital recording also spawned the development of a new format for recorded music. Invented in 1979, the compact disc looked convincingly futuristic: shiny, silver and supposedly immune to scratching or other kinds of residual degradation that plagued vinyl records over repeated plays, and able to deliver around 80 minutes of sharply detailed, crackle-free sonic reproduction.

THRASH METAL COMES OF AGE

MASTER OF PUPPETS
METALLICA
1986

Metallica's debut *Kill 'Em All* (1983) married hardcore punk's velocity to the riffs, aggression and musicianship of Motörhead and New Wave of British Heavy Metal (NWOBHM) bands. ('Metallica's whole vibe came from Diamond Head,' Lars Ulrich told *MOJO* in 2007. 'Fast heavy metal, unorthodox arrangements, and that aura of arrogance.') *Ride the Lightning* (1984) honed their signature sound, which had nothing to do with metal's penchant for fantasy or contemporary 'hair metal' bands such as Bon Jovi and Ratt. But with apologies to Slayer's *Reign in Blood* of the same year, *Master of Puppets* stands tall as thrash-metal's most influential masterpiece.

By their third album, Metallica had become a band open to experimentation without sacrificing the menacing riffs, eye-popping speed and ferocious aural assault that made them. The songs are longer than on previous albums, epic in proportion, texturally nuanced. The gentle acoustic guitar prelude on 'Battery' is, of course, a deceptive curtain-raiser. A minute in, the track takes off at 190 bpm, in a blistering yowl of pride for the underground San Francisco metal scene that birthed Metallica.

'Disposable Heroes' – a hymn to human cannon fodder – is eight-minutes-plus of tempo shifts, with ferocious strumming mimicking military drumbeats; its theme is picked up for the album cover. Who needed fantasy evils when humanity's foibles offered such rich pickings? Elsewhere, prodigiously gifted bassist Cliff Burton (who was to die in a road accident while the band were touring the LP) plays engrossing lead bass on the brooding shape-shifter 'Orion'.

The album's sole single, 'Master of Puppets', tackles addiction – inspired by junkies that frontman and lyricist James Hetfield came across at a party, though he later made a connection with his own alcoholism. Powerlessness of one sort or another runs through the set like an open wound. 'Damage Inc.' – featuring stop-start rhythms at a barely believable rate – ends the set with more breakneck mayhem, this time a malevolent, mindlessly destructive agency with the listener in its sights.

Airplay? Zilch – a reflection of what radio stations and the press thought of thrash metal at a time when poodle-haired rockers were in the ascendance. It's testament to Metallica's devoted and growing following that the album made the US Top 30, eventually going six times platinum. In terms of inspiration, though, it's off the charts. In 2021, Slipknot's Corey Taylor told Knotfest.com that it was 'the perfect heavy metal album. There's no fat.'

James Hetfield and Kirk Hemmett get shredding at the Poplar Creek Music Theater in Illinois, in 1986

ACID IN THE HOUSE: RAVE

In the mid-80s, DJs in Chicago began evolving pared-down, four-to-the floor beats, hard, hypnotic and repetitive– often generated by a Roland TR-909 drum machine – with snippets of vocals rather than full verses and choruses. And a squelchy bassline created by twiddling with the modulation on Roland's TB-303 synth/sequencer – a commercial flop, its budget price made it affordable to creative minds within the city's poorer communities and enabled non-musicians to start making music. Echoes there of hip-hop's fledgling years.

Among its pioneers were DJ Pierre (aka Nathaniel Jones), partner Earl 'Spanky' Smith and Herbert 'Herb J' Jackson. Having taped one track, they took it to Ron Hardy, who played it at the city's Music Box club, where an initially muted reaction gave way to increasing enthusiasm after repeated plays. With production input from Marshall Jefferson, the trio (as Phuture) released the track in 1987: 'Acid Tracks' became a cornerstone of acid house, to be joined by the likes of Armando's mesmerizingly simple '151'.

UK acid house and dance culture generally took off big time after a group of British DJs including Danny Rampling, Paul Oakenfold and Mike Pickering went clubbing in Ibiza in 1987. They returned brimming with enthusiasm for DJ Alfredo Fiorillo's anything-goes sets at the open-aired Amnesia, along with Chicago's acid house. Back home, they started organizing Balearic nights.

The DJs' evangelistic enthusiasm for the new music was also informed by the drug MDMA, or Ecstasy. It induced a rush of warmth and loved-up sensations, amplified the music's trance-like qualities and inspired a sense of communality that (briefly) united even rival football hooligans, who extended their pill-popping to match days. Black, gay disco-goers had dropped E in the 1970s, but by 1988 it had crossed over to a new generation of UK house music lovers, who packed out all-night dance parties ('raves') – often in abandoned warehouses, as licensed premises wouldn't cater to all-night sessions – in the summers of '88 and '89.

Acid daze at London's all-nighter Shoom in 1988

Ravers followed underground, word-of-mouth instructions and pirate radio, to track down venues. Acid had its own look – the ubiquitous smiley face on T-shirts (as featured on the third flyer for Rampling's club Shoom – named for an E's rush), beanie hats and baggy clothes, day-glo colours and glowsticks.

By April 1988, S'Express's 'Theme from S'Express' made UK no.1. Manchester's Haçienda inaugurated its midweek acid-house 'Hot' night three months later. In 2001's *Pump Up the Volume*, the club's co-founder Tony Wilson recalled his sudden realization that the sea change in pop brought about by the Beatles at the Cavern in 1962, and Sex Pistols' appearance at Manchester's Lesser Free Trade Hall in 1976, was again in the air.

Those illegal parties drew the ire of the tabloid press. The Entertainments (Increased Penalties) Act 1990 hit rave promoters with stringent fines. Four years later, the infamous Criminal Justice and Public Order Act outlawed gatherings that featured music 'wholly or predominantly characterized by the emission of a succession of repetitive beats'. Not since Sex Pistols' 'God Save the Queen' had popular music clashed so openly with the British establishment.

A HIP-HOP BOMB

IT TAKES A NATION OF MILLIONS TO HOLD US BACK
PUBLIC ENEMY
1988

'"The Message" gave a platform to every single rap group that came afterwards, including Public Enemy,' PE's mastermind Chuck D told *MOJO* in 2007. But the voice on that epochal single by Grandmaster Flash and the Furious Five is worn down, borderline psychotic. On *It Takes a Nation of Millions to Hold Us Back*, Public Enemy sound anything but.

This is focused rage. Articulate passion. A resurrection of pride reminiscent of the Black Panthers and shaped by that movement's provocative stance (the Panthers' militaristic garb inspired PE's 'Security of the First World' cohorts, who performed mock-military drills with toy rifles on stage). A swipe at America's Black middle class, seen as all too keen to blend in, coupled with a clarion call for political re-engagement. Hip-hop with punk's hell-for-leather urgency – Public Enemy, as has been noted, crossing Run-DMC with the Clash. 'We looked at ourselves as media dispatchers,' Chuck D told Q in 2007. 'A great antenna, the ultimate in pirate radio.'

As MC, Chuck D's flow is stream-of-consciousness constant, berating, accusing, informing. Flavor Flav plays court jester, injecting the narrative with irreverent asides and jokes, a counterbalance to what might become overwhelming rhetoric. 'Don't Believe the Hype' snipered the negative press that had dogged the group since their 1987 debut *Yo! Bum Rush the Show*, while 'Bring the Noise' called out other (unnamed) critics, asserted rap's claims for legitimacy as an art form, and pre-emptively struck at radio stations who would refuse to play the track – a theme that resurfaced on the album's centrepiece.

Released as a taster single, 'Rebel Without a Pause' set the tone for *It Takes a Nation of Millions*, from its punning title to the game-changing production, featuring a squealing sax sample from James Brown's 'The Grunt' that became the band's sonic stamp. The track set PE apart from the rap pack in other ways, notably its 109 bpm speed – faster than most hip-hop – but also in its assertion of PE's group mentality: they were a crew. Nearly 20 years later, Chuck insisted to Q, 'I don't rate myself at all. I'm a member of a team.'

'She Watch Channel Zero?!' nails addiction to junk TV, just as 1991's '1 Million Bottlebags' would address alcoholism among the Black community, driven by biased advertising, and 'Night of the Living Baseheads' engaged with the crack-cocaine epidemic that devastated Black communities in the mid-1980s. 'Caught, Can We Get a Witness?' picks up on the cost of clearing copyrights for samples – something that struck at the core of hip-hop's liberal mix'n'match policy – but maintains that as artists of colour created most of them in the first

Professor Griff, Flavor Flav, Terminator X, Chuck D and the S1W 'security' posse bring the noise, circa 1988

BEATS AND THE BEATEN GENERATION 1977–1999

place, PE should be permitted to re-use them. ('Night of the Living Baseheads' alone employs around 20 samples, including a speech by Nation of Islam's Khalid Muhammad.) 'Party for Your Right to Fight' is a smart reworking of the breakthrough hit by Beastie Boys – PE's labelmates at Def Jam – though Chuck D explained it as a Black Panthers tribute.

Run-DMC might have got there earlier, but Public Enemy incorporate rock into their aural avalanches here too, sampling 'Angel of Death' from Slayer's classic *Reign in Blood* (1986). And after Anthrax – part of thrash metal's Big Four, along with Slayer, Metallica and Megadeth – covered 'Bring the Noise', PE wound up on tour with them, the two acts coming together to close out each night with the track.

The album's dense textures set the oppressive, provocative tone, an intense collage of samples concocted by avant-garde in-house production wizards the Bomb Squad – headed up by Hank Shocklee, brothers Keith and Eric Sadler – and DJ Terminator X's deck skills. 'Years of saved-up ideas were compiled into one focused aural missile,' Chuck D revealed to *MOJO* in 1995, one that blew hip-hop's parameters wide open. He sent advance copies to, among others, Dr Dre and Ice T in Los Angeles, and something of its pointed ire found its way onto NWA's *Straight Outta Compton*, released two months later. The album's proud Black nationalism merged with the Afrocentrism of A Tribe Called Quest. Beastie Boy Adam Yauch praised Chuck D as 'the most important MC in hip-hop' to *Rolling Stone* in 2004, both for his delivery and his content.

In October 1988, *NME* made Chuck and Co. cover stars, under the headline 'Public Enemy. The greatest rock'n'roll band in the world?!' Right then, no doubt about it.

'I JUST SAT IN THE PARK AND LISTENED TO THAT RECORD FOR FOUR HOURS. AND I SAID TO MYSELF, THIS IS WHAT I WANT TO DO WITH MY LIFE.'

QUESTLOVE

With 1983's 'It's Like That' – pared down to no-nonsense voice and beatbox – Run-DMC gave hip-hop an edge and street-wise image, while 1986's multi-platinum *Raising Hell* LP proved that it had commercial clout. Although divisive at the time, a collaboration with Stonesy rockers Aerosmith on the latter's 'Walk This Way' inaugurated the rock-rap crossover with a Transatlantic Top 10 hit (though they'd laced rap with rock guitar on 1985's 'King of Rock'). The Beastie Boys' frat-party antics did something similar on 'Fight For Your Right to Party', from *Licensed to Ill*, rap's first *Billboard* no.1.

De La Soul's joyous *Three Feet High and Rising* celebrated the genre's power for positivity – seconded by spiritual brothers A Tribe Called Quest – while Salt-N-Pepa provided the genre with much-needed forceful female perspective (see 1988's 'Push It'). Starting with 1987's 'Rebel Without a Pause', Public Enemy (like Run-DMC and Beastie Boys, both on the Def Jam label) honed articulate, aggressive releases with outrageous production. NWA (Niggaz With Attitude) stoked up the provocation on the fiery *Straight Outta Compton*, notably with 'Fuck Tha Police'. Cue gang-referencing, braggadocio-heavy gangsta rap.

With 1993's *Enter the Wu-Tang (36 Chambers)*, nine-strong supergroup Wu-Tang Clan channelled violent imagery, gritty production and warped humour to create a defining sound for 90s hardcore hip hop. But the brilliance of artists such as Snoop Dogg, Tupac Shakur and the Notorious BIG played out against internecine rap wars – East vs West Coast, Sean 'Puffy' Combs's Bad Boy Records vs Suge Knight's Death Row.

In the 21st century, high-profile rappers such as Dre protégé Eminem, Jay-Z and Kanye West, in tandem with powerhouse team Missy Elliott and producer Timbaland, and the provocative Nicki Minaj, saw rap become part of pop's lingua franca, a global institution that overtook rock as the most popular music in America in 2017.

POP'S QUEEN OF CONTROVERSY HAS HER DEFINING MOMENT

'LIKE A PRAYER'
MADONNA
1989

Sex and religion: a combustible mix, as Madonna Louise Ciccone knew well. In 1985, she'd brazenly informed *SPIN* that 'Crucifixes are sexy because there's a naked man on them,' but also, 'If I wasn't doing what I'm doing, I would be a nun.' A year earlier, she'd popped eyes with erotic capers on the MTV Music Video Awards stage, in a white wedding dress. That was 'Like a Virgin'. But 'Like a Prayer' was something else entirely.

The song's allusive lyrics toy with double meaning and are open to (mis)interpretation. It could be a declaration of spiritual devotion in terms that might also be applied to romantic love. Madonna herself stated that it was the song of someone in love with God, who thus becomes the most important male figure in her life.

That God sometimes reaches out to her in the dead of the night inevitably recalls the imagery of a sexually alive song like Wilson Pickett's 'In the Midnight Hour'. Then again, our deepest worries often visit us at that time too – so is this a plea for spiritual help, which God answers? But what about taking him (or Him) 'there' – the Staple Singers did that in a song run through with spiritual joy, but mightn't it also imply something carnal? Then again, Andraé Crouch's gospel choir, who close the song out so euphorically – that's simply an open-hearted declaration of faith and God's love... right? Crouch thought so: he'd scrutinized the lyrics before agreeing to participate. But once he understood what Madonna planned for the video, he declined to have his choir take part.

Unprecedentedly, the world got to hear a taster of Madonna's new single – on 22 February 1989 – in a commercial for her sponsor Pepsi, who'd signed her just two months previously in a $5-million deal. Ten days later, the world saw a two-minute version. And the day after that, the world got the full video, which brews up a cauldron of provocative imagery: the wrongful arrest of a Black man for murdering a white girl; stigmata appearing on Madonna's palms; an array of burning crosses aflame at night. And at its heart, the singer kissing an animated statue of a Black saint (identified by many viewers as Jesus). Sometimes we need our pop to be provocative, to expose uneasy truths, and not just those about religion. Those scenes resurrected the historic taboo of a white woman becoming intimate with a Black man, and the repercussions – for him.

'I wanted to speak about ecstasy and to show the relationship between sexual and religious ecstasy,' the video's director, Mary Lambert, later revealed

MADONNA

LIKE A PRAYER

Madonna takes it to church

to *Rolling Stone*. To the *Hollywood Reporter*, Lambert also singled out those flaming crosses as an act of usurpation – 'the Ku Klux Klan could take a cross, which is a holy symbol to a lot of people, and appropriate it in a way to instil fear and horror and promote race hatred'.

Whatever the background conceptualizing, it's fair to say that the video got a reaction. The Vatican was up in arms: 'The video is a blasphemy and insult,' seethed Roman Catholic historian Roberto de Mattei, 'because it shows immorals inside a church.' Pope John Paul II encouraged Italian Madonna fans to shun the singer's *Blond Ambition* tour, and the Vatican boycotted both Pepsi and its subsidiaries (including Kentucky Fried Chicken and Pizza Hut) – a little unfair, as Pepsi weren't directly involved in the offending video. The soft drinks conglomerate – who couldn't really boycott the Vatican – dropped the video after two airings, and then dropped Madonna.

Record buyers didn't share the Catholic Church's reservations: the single went on to spend three weeks at the top of *Billboard*'s Hot 100. The video was subsequently voted the most ground-breaking of all time by viewers on the occasion of MTV's 25th anniversary, and whetted appetites for Madonna's *Like a Prayer* album – one of her finest – which became her third *Billboard* No.1, shifting some 15 million units and spawning four US Top 10 hits.

Sex and religion. It's an itch that Madonna can't resist scratching. For 2006's *Confessions* tour, she appeared open-armed on a crucifix, her brow framed by a fake crown of thorns. 'The Catholic Church *needs* to have a stick poked at it, for God sakes,' she insisted to *MOJO* in 2015.

'I WASN'T SITTING THERE IN MY LABORATORY OF S***-STIRRING, GOING, "OOH THIS IS GONNA F*** WITH PEOPLE".'

MADONNA

Launched on 1 August 1981 with Buggles' 'Video Killed the Radio Star', cable channel MTV transformed the way we access music and drove the rise of the music video as a promotional tool. It coincided with a resurgence of glamorous pop and a wave of visually striking British New Romantic artists such as Duran Duran, Spandau Ballet and Culture Club, who proved a dream match for the new format. Along with New Wave of British Heavy Metal front-runners such as Def Leppard, they heralded a mini 'Second British Invasion' Stateside.

But MTV's rock-biased programming soon attracted flak, not least because white artists dominated. Even Michael Jackson struggled for airtime: released on 2 January 1983, his 'Billie Jean' video only gained 'medium rotation' at MTV once it had already topped the *Billboard* chart. In its wake, however, a turnaround began, with releases by major Black artists such as Prince, Lionel Richie and Donna Summer put into heavy rotation.

The 14-minute, $1-million mini film for Jackson's 'Thriller' shook things up again, redefining video and kick-starting its commercial market; in its wake, Black artists gained more of a foothold on MTV. The track's astronomically successful parent album also proved a game-changer for the music business – and not just because of its all-conquering sales (though they provided a much-needed boost, with the industry suffering two slumps in three years). Of its nine tracks, *Thriller* yielded seven US Top 10 hit singles, ushering in a new era in promotion and marketing, with campaigns that might be sustained for a couple of years built around a single LP. Mid-1980s blockbusters *Born in the USA* (Bruce Springsteen), *Purple Rain* (Prince) and *Like a Virgin* (Madonna) all owed a debt to *Thriller*.

GRUNGE'S BREAKOUT ALBUM REDEFINES ROCK

NEVERMIND
NIRVANA
1991

In a famous quote, actor James Dean once suggested that he thought he'd make it because he had Montgomery Clift in one hand saying 'help me' and Marlon Brando in the other saying 'screw you'. Something of those mixed messages resurfaced in Kurt Cobain and Nirvana's momentous *Nevermind*. In Brando's court were the group's blistering sonic assaults ('Breed', 'Territorial Pissings', 'Stay Away'). But the album's penultimate track, the emotionally bereft 'Something in the Way', is Clift territory.

Cobain once famously summed up Nirvana's signature sound as 'the Knack and the Bay City Rollers being molested by Black Flag and Black Sabbath', and thought his songs' loud-quiet-loud dynamic all too obviously in thrall to Pixies and college-radio staples Hüsker Dü. None of that explains *Nevermind*'s impact, both commercial (sales of 10-million-plus) and cultural. The whirlwind of sound – metal merged with punk mayhem – propelled by ex-hardcore drummer Dave Grohl. The deadpan lyrics, affecting disinterest, that made Cobain (unwillingly) the voice of the lost 'Generation X', and his own throat-lacerating scream – of boredom, pain, weakness. A man, as was said of Nick Drake, with one skin too few. And crucially, *Nevermind* was a work of focus – from Cobain's crafted punk-pop songs and the band's road-hardened tightness, to Butch Vig's punchy production and no-fat nous. Suddenly, rock giants such as Guns N' Roses – Nirvana's Geffen labelmates – seemed passé.

The foot in the door was the opening track. 'I don't think *Nevermind* would have been *Nevermind* without "Smells Like Teen Spirit",' mused Jonathan Poneman – co-founder of the Sub Pop label that released Nirvana debut *Bleach* – to *MOJO* 20 years after the album's release. Exhibiting an ambivalence characteristic of its composer, its surreal, allusive lyrics both display and deplore the apathy with which Cobain's generation was identified. But there's nothing ambivalent about the whomp of the band, the riff that hooks you from the off, or the enticing uneasiness beneath it all (something reflected in the album's cover: a waterborne baby reaching for a dollar bill). It made the *Billboard* Top 5; meantime, the album was going stratospheric, CD pressing plants unable to meet demand, gigs packed out with screaming fans. An underground sound, forged in a small town in Washington State, had gone exponentially overground.

On 11 January 1992, *Nevermind* displaced Michael Jackson's *Dangerous* as *Billboard*'s No.1 album.

Cobain at London's Astoria in 1991, sporting his Lead Belly sweatshirt

BEATS AND THE BEATEN GENERATION 1977–1999

AVANT-GARDE ELECTRO MASTERPIECE

SELECTED AMBIENT WORKS 85–92
APHEX TWIN
1992

In *Ocean of Sound* (2001), David Toop relates that Richard D. 'Aphex Twin' James once informed him, 'I just like music that sounds evil or eerie.' He certainly revels in confounding expectations and messing with minds, from the nightmarishly brutal 'Come to Daddy' (with its equally disturbing video) and glitch-beat weirdness of 'Rubber Johnny', to the remorseless clatter of 'Didgeridoo'. This is the man who played sandpaper and a food blender at London's Garage club. But along with mischievous aural muggings, he's equally capable of conjuring up captivating beauty. And in 1992, he released a collection of tracks, the earliest recorded in his mid-teens, that *Fact* magazine later acclaimed as the greatest of its decade and which became a wellspring for intelligent dance music (IDM).

Save for the hushed 'i', this isn't quite ambience in the tradition of Brian Eno's *Thursday Afternoon*, Nils Frahm's *Felt* or Max Richter's *Sleep*. James's techno sensibilities hover just in sight, and a spellbinding range of beats add grains of grit to these slowly shifting clouds of sound. Opener 'Xtal' blends metallic-sounding percussion into a female chorus and synth wash. A fruity acid bass line and spitting electro intrusions speck the gorgeous theme of 'Green Calx'. Vocals, when they do appear, are swallowed in reverb – soft-edged and amorphous. But so deeply diverse are James's percussive tonalities that they take on ambiences of their own. Indeed, one of the album's singular features is its rich variety of textures, among which is a recurring hiss – many tracks were taken directly from cassette-tape demos – although this comes across less as an imperfection than an entirely sympathetic aural effect.

Every tune is concisely structured, decorated with hooks and always stimulating. Most could be pop songs shorn of lead vocals, some are even playful. But others – such as 'Ageispolis' or 'Hedphelym' – engrossing though they are, feel like excursions into the desolate sonic hinterlands later staked out by Boards of Canada.

James was curious and technically gifted from childhood, reportedly 'preparing' the family's piano in a Cageian way long before discovering John Cage himself. He'd tinker with tape recorders or adjust the pre-set frequencies on his

The seldom-seen Richard D. James tinkers with the parameters of dance music

Roland SH-101 synth, pushing them into sub- and supersonic ranges – a maverick artist-producer in the tradition of Joe Meek.

Selected Ambient Works 85–92 flits between recognizable genres without settling, tempting you to define it before sliding free. Much like its composer, around whom an enticing aura of mystery and mythology still hovers, 30 years after the release of this lodestar in electronic music.

BEATS AND THE BEATEN GENERATION 1977–1999

PIONEERING FEMALE-FRONTED HIP-HOP RELEASE

SUPA DUPA FLY
MISSY ELLIOTT
1997

Hip-hop, like rock, was too long dominated by male artists, with women put down or assigned walk-on parts as sex objects. If that's less true today, much of the credit goes to inspirational creative individualists such as Missy Elliott. And much of that is down to her debut, *Supa Dupa Fly*.

In producer Timbaland – a friend from high school – she had an experimentalist after her own heart, one who mixed-and-matched offbeat arrangements, out-of-the-box rhythms and hooks, horns and electronic slow jams to complement her sometimes surreal lyrics. The previous year, the duo served as a songwriter/producer team for nine tracks on Aaliyah's double-platinum *One in a Million*, including four hit singles, so they had industry form by the time they began work on *Supa Dupa Fly*.

No cartoons here: in song and rap, Elliott explores the complexities of being a contemporary Black woman. She's sexually avaricious on 'Sock it 2 Me' and 'Beep Me 911', but vulnerable too, seeking explanation from errant partners, taking stock of female friendships ('Best Friends', a home-girls heart-to-heart with Aaliyah), breaking hearts and having hers broken. And in an era still reeling from the murders of Tupac Shakur and the Notorious BIG the previous year, and tit-for-tat rap wars between East and West Coast, she had the coolness to stayed focused and light: 'Her whole thing was "I gotta do this and make it fun",' Timbaland reflected to TheUndefeated.com in 2017.

The futuristic vibe that characterizes much of the production is complemented by Hype Williams's singular videos – a major contribution to the Missy image. For 'The Rain (Supa Dupa Fly)' she's a blimped-up, black-clad Michelin Woman, exploding her natural curves exponentially; at times, her lips cover the camera's fish-eye lens. Fun and then some, and flirtatious, but never pandering to the male gaze.

In the 'Sock it 2 Me' video, she's a spacehero battling robotic nemeses alongside Lil' Kim – with whom she partners on 'Hit 'Em wit da Hee' – then ceding screen time to a mile-a-minute delivery from female rapper Da Brat. Affirmative, celebratory and a universe away from the hissy spats involving Lil' Kim and fellow raunch rapper Foxy Brown. (Timbaland roundly praised Elliott as a champion of creatively simpatico female artists.) In a time when hip-hop seemed to be ripping itself apart, maybe space, or an Afrocentric future world, felt like the best place.

Outsized talent: Missy in 1998

BEATS AND THE BEATEN GENERATION 1977–1999

A J-POP MAGNUM OPUS

FANTASMA
CORNELIUS
1997

Perhaps as part of a *fin de siècle* retrospection, the 1990s saw a revival of interest in music long dismissed as unforgivably kitsch, such as easy listening and cocktail music. In Japanese pop (J-pop), a related micro-genre called Shibuya-kei emerged that, among other things, drew on the sunshine pop of the Beach Boys and Brian Wilson's baroque productions, French yé-yé girls, and the popcraft of Burt Bacharach and Hal David. *Fantasma* was not only a stunning expansion of that ethos, but pivotal in arousing interest in J-pop among Western listeners.

Cornelius (aka Keigo Oyamada) has Wilson's loving devotion to sonic detail. Opener 'Mic Check' sets the tone: the snap of a cigarette lighter, a can popping open, the rustle of a wrapper, and Cornelius asks '*Kikoemasu ka?*' ('Can you hear me?'). An audiophile preparing his ground. What follows is a whirlwind of samples and pastiche – not unlike searching through the stations on an analogue radio. On 'Chapter 8 (Seashore and Horizon)', a gentle singalong from psych poppers Apples in Stereo abruptly clicks off, giving way to a gorgeous 'answering' snippet from Cornelius. Another click, a tape rewinds and we're back with Apples in Stereo. Then it does it again – shades of the carefree experimentation of Os Mutantes' debut album (see p.80), a spiritual ancestor to *Fantasma*.

'Star Fruits Surf Rider' pairs gentle tropicália with drum and bass clatter, anticipating Cornelius's 1999 remix of Blur's 'Tender'. 'Count Five or Six' must be heard on headphones to appreciate its full stereophonic glory. The range of samples would have delighted *Odelay-era* Beck (with whom Cornelius was compared) or the *Paul's Boutique* Beastie Boys, from a 1950s cartoon soundtrack and 60s hi-fi demo record, to Sex Pistols' 'God Save the Queen'. There are five in 'Magoo Opening' alone – all 128 seconds of it.

To quote a sample beloved of late 80s hip-hop, this is a journey into sound – one best heard straight through. Repeated listens reveal apparent randomness to be painstaking programming. Elements in 'Mic Check' recur throughout the album that follows: the faint Beach Boys-like song turns out to be the album's eponymous closing track; the robot-speak countdown returns for 'Count Five or Six'. The penultimate 'Thank You For the Music' incorporates a collage-like reprise of previous tracks.

That all this comes across as off-the-cuff colourful, fresh and fun is astounding. No wonder it ends with the sound of a deep intake of breath.

The spectral Cornelius, in a giveaway picture included with *Fantasma*

BEATS AND THE BEATEN GENERATION 1977–1999

NAPSTER, STREAMING AND THE MUSIC INDUSTRY

In 1999, teenager Shawn Fanning launched peer-to-peer sharing site Napster. Anyone connected to a network of interlinked computers could instantly (and illegally) download music for free; by 2000, Napster had around 100 million users. In April 2001, Metallica took Napster to court; Dr Dre followed suit (they even shared the same attorney). 'Metallica fans sided with Napster because they're lazy bastards and they want everything for free,' guitarist James Hetfield complained the following year. 'I like playing music because it's a good living and I get satisfaction from it but I can't feed my family with satisfaction.' Napster settled both lawsuits, axed its free file-sharing practices and, by 2002, declared bankruptcy.

But the digital genie was out of the bottle, and the following year Apple's iTunes store opened for download purchases; 'Crazy' by Gnarls Barkley became the first download-only UK No.1 in 2006. Had record companies – which had overcharged customers and underpaid artists for decades – engaged with Napster's model instead of trying to run it out of town, they might have developed subscribed copyright-friendly download services earlier.

Among a host of repercussions, Napster's outrageous success raised the prospect of a divorce in the previously harmonious marriage between artist and fan. Artists liked the album format and understandably wanted to be paid for their work. 'I'd really much rather write a novel than a bunch of short stories,' Taylor Swift told Yahoo in 2014. 'Albums defined my childhood, and they've defined my life.' Fans, however, were increasingly more likely to cherry-pick tracks rather than buy a whole album, and many were happy to take their heroes' music gratis. So was the album now suddenly redundant? (Contrarily, Arctic Monkeys actively encouraged free file-sharing and gave away CDs at gigs – DIY marketing concepts that helped their meteoric rise in the early 2000s, with little public promotion.)

Innovations in music technology come round ever more rapidly, and the CD proved to be popular music's last physical format. Music had become portable since the appearance of the transistor radio in the 1950s, running through the cassette and CD Walkman. In 2001, Apple released the first iPod. By 2007 it had shifted 100 million units to become history's highest-selling digital music player. But its heyday was brief: as of 2019, only the iPod Touch was still in production.

The main reason for this was that buy-to-own downloads had given way to streamed music. Subscription-based streaming services were to prove a lifeline for the music industry; not so for musicians. Outraged by the niggardly payback, Taylor Swift removed her music from Spotify in 2014 and demanded that she be remunerated properly for her work. Perhaps it's a sign of how ubiquitous such services are, though, that after three years she made her catalogue Spotifiable again. Streaming has been particularly ungenerous to musicians, especially in the wake of the Covid-19 pandemic, when live performance was curtailed. By 2019, nearly 80 per cent of all music was streamed, but the royalties that artists earn from them are beggarly – just $0.003 per stream on Spotify as of October 2021, or 300 streams to make $1. And this from the world's largest music-streaming provider, with more than 380 million monthly users.

In 2014, Apple belatedly bought into the subscription model by purchasing Beats Music (co-founded by Dr Dre and Interscope Records founder Jimmy Iovine) and turning it into Apple Music. The next year, streaming service Tidal was rebooted with a host of high-profile co-stakeholders, including Jay-Z (its prime mover), Beyoncé, Madonna, Rihanna and Kanye West. It was a company co-owned by artists, which pledged to properly remunerate musicians, albeit with a monthly subscription fee twice that of Spotify. But with West jumping ship in 2017, and disquiet over alleged manipulation of listener figures, its model remains unproven.

One thing *is* certain. With the vinyl revival small scale, and CDs and downloads in steady decline, the world is set to stream on.

INVENTION
AND
DISSENSION

2000—PRESENT

That the internet has revolutionized the way we think about, and consume, music is a given. Launched at the start of the 21st century, Napster posed an unprecedented threat to the record industry: unlawful file-streaming, followed by the advent of Apple's digital-friendly iPods and iTunes store helped send once inviolable institutions such as Tower Records into a swift death dive.

The music industry is a slow-moving behemoth, but gradually adapted: downloads, and more significantly streaming, offered a lifeline and potential future. That said, Radiohead's Thom Yorke was not alone in his vitriol towards the biggest streamer of them all, Spotify, describing it to Mexico's Sopitas website in 2013 as 'the last desperate fart of a dying corpse' and decrying its cosy relationship with major labels. Fans shared music and video via platforms such as Facebook, Twitter and latterly TikTok, thereby introducing new opportunities for artists and producers to promote their work.

One of the most refreshing aspects of the new century was the continuing rise of creative, independent women such as Missy Elliott, whose partnership with producer Timbaland recalibrated hip-hop with stripped down releases such as 'Get Ur Freak On', and a grab-bag of ideas from psyche to Bollywood soundtracks. OutKast's success, epitomized by 2003's stellar 'Hey Ya!' and its parent *Speakerboxxx/The Love Below* album, reacquainted hip-hop with funk, rock'n'roll, R&B and soul.

With the advent of sampling, pop's recorded history became an open library to explore. Indeed, so long has contemporary music been engaged in a post-post-modern conversation with the past that turning influences into inspirational new forms takes a truly original mind. One example might be Lady Gaga, who brought an art-world spirit of pastiche and high concept to a series of bestselling albums.

The gritty street sounds of the UK's grime scene simmered underground until major talents including Dizzee Rascal, So Solid Crew – and later Skepta and Stormzy – sent it chartwards. Stormzy in particular has used it to make highly political, establishment-challenging statements – backed up by practical interventions to boost education and literacy.

Reliably controversial, politically unpredictable and musically prodigious, Kanye West has provided some of the century's stand-out pop. Elsewhere, the Dr Dre-mentored Eminem rode on waves of controversy – homophobia, and misogynistic lyrics sometimes bordering on the horrific – to become the rap Elvis. The rise of West, alongside that of similarly inspired figures such as Jay-Z, saw rap become the most popular music in the USA in the 2010s; West and Jay-Z both headlined Glastonbury Festival, to the chagrin of some (such as Oasis's Noel Gallagher), who thought rock's territory should be preserved like a heritage site.

Garage rock got a revival with the drums-and-guitar-what-more-do-you-need White Stripes. And of the wave of new female singer-songwriters, few were finer than Amy Winehouse, who brought a deep respect for doo wop, R&B and soul – and a fatalism tempered with sly wit – to 2006's iconic *Back to Black*.

A rash of serious sexual abuse accusations levelled at high-profile figures such as Hollywood producer Harvey Weinstein and rapper R. Kelly were the background to a new movement championing women speaking up and bringing male exploitation to task: #MeToo. Acceptance of the breadth and fluidity of the sexual landscape, in the form of the LGBTQ+ community, was reflected in exceptional releases by the likes of Janelle Monáe (2010's *The ArchAndroid*, 2013's 'Q.U.E.E.N.') and Christine and the Queens (2014's *Chaleur Humaine*, 2018's *Chris*), while Frank Ocean's success helped chip away at rap's gnarly, homophobic edges, producing two of the century's standouts in *channel ORANGE* (2012) and *Blonde* (2016).

In tandem, racial disparity and violence against people of colour (as highlighted by a series of deaths of Black individuals at the hands of white policemen) prompted street marches, riots and protests – notably in sports and song. The divisive US presidency of Donald Trump encapsulated the grievous tensions within his country. Pop took to the barricades, with outspoken albums by the likes of Kendrick Lamar and the mighty Beyoncé, who took the Black Panthers' revolutionary spirit to the all-American spectacle of the Super Bowl in 2016.

'I WANT YOU TO KNOW THAT YOU MATTER, I WANT YOU TO KNOW THAT YOUR LIVES MATTER, THAT YOUR DREAMS MATTER.'

FORMER US PRESIDENT BARACK OBAMA
ON GEORGE FLOYD AND POLICE BRUTALITY

2001
→ On 11 September, two planes hijacked by members of al-Qaeda fly into the Twin Towers of New York's World Trade Center. Two other airliners are also hijacked, one of which strikes the Pentagon. Nearly 3,000 people lose their lives, the majority during the New York attacks.
→ Apple launches the iPod.
→ Wikipedia is founded.

2003
→ US/UK-led invasion of Iraq begins.
→ Co-founded by Mark Zuckerberg, Facebook is launched. By 2017 it will have 2 billion users worldwide.

2004
→ Arrival of two NASA Mars Exploration Rovers on the 'Red Planet'.

2005
→ Hurricane Katrina devastates the south-eastern USA.
→ Terrorist attacks hit London, killing 52 people and injuring a further 700.

2006
→ Arctic Monkeys' *Whatever People Say I Am, That's What I'm Not* becomes the fastest-selling debut album by a band in British chart history.
→ Spotify and Twitter are both founded.

2007
→ A global economic crisis starts to unfold, prompted in part by the collapse of the US sub-prime mortgage market. US stock market will eventually fall by around 50 per cent.
→ Apple launches the iPhone.
→ The UN estimates that for the first time most of the world's population is now living in urban areas.

2009
→ Barack Obama becomes the 44th US president and first Black incumbent of the White House.

2010
→ The 'Arab Spring' – a string of demonstrations and protests – emerges in the Middle East.

2011

→   Beginning of the Syrian Civil War.

2012

→   Hilary Mantel wins an unprecedented second Booker Prize.

2014

→   Launch of the Tidal streaming service.

→   Taylor Swift pulls her back catalogue from Spotify.

2015

→   Same-sex marriage is legalized throughout the USA.

→   Terrorist attacks shock Paris.

→   In a move by the International Federation of the Phonographic Industry to tackle piracy, global music release day shifts to Friday.

2016

→   The UK votes to leave the European Union.

2017

→   Donald Trump elected 45th US president.

→   For the first time, streaming takes over as the biggest revenue earner for the US music industry.

2018

→   Apple becomes the first company to be valued at $1 trillion.

→   Kendrick Lamar wins a Pulitzer Prize for his 2017 album *DAMN*.

→   Cardi B becomes the first female rapper to have two US No.1 singles, with 'I Like It' and 'Bodak Yellow'.

2019

→   An outbreak of the Covid-19 virus. In March 2020, the World Health Organization declares it a pandemic.

→   K-Pop boy band BTS get the coveted role of kicking off the *Good Morning America* summer concerts.

2020

→   Black US citizen George Floyd dies when a police officer kneels on his neck and back for nine and a half minutes. Amid the international outrage, it becomes a defining event for the Black Lives Matter movement.

CRITICS' DARLINGS CONFOUND EXPECTATIONS

KID A
RADIOHEAD
2000

Their previous set, *OK Computer* (1997), introduced prog-rock shape-shifters like 'Paranoid Android' in a commercial and artistic triumph that Q magazine's readers giddily voted the best album of all time. But Radiohead – especially lead singer Thom Yorke – baulked at fame's onerous tolls and expectations.

Kid A is the sound of a band leaving *OK Computer*'s sunny path for the dark woods. Something closer to the uncertain, elusive electronica characteristic of Warp Records, floating worlds of disembodied voices and aural shadows. But as Yorke himself observed, it's also an insight into the fraught limboland in which the band found themselves, shell-shocked by success. 'Kid A' and 'Idioteque' reference the kind of eerie intelligent dance music (IDM) produced by Warp artists such as Aphex Twin and Boards of Canada. Yorke's distinctive vocals, hitherto a constant from breakthrough hit 'Creep' to 'The Tourist', *OK Computer*'s closing track, are submerged by brass on 'The National Anthem', or fractured and disfigured ('Kid A' again), just another instrument in the mix.

You like verse-chorus-verse? Look elsewhere. *Kid A* loves texture and timbre, the nuances of sound, skittery beats and tricksy time signatures. A collective writer's block actually helped here – untypically, the band had to build songs up in the studio, from sketchy aural snippets. Guitars don't sound like guitars – on 'Morning Bell', Jonny Greenwood scrapes a coin along his strings. Instruments uncommon in rock, notably the ondes Martenot, disrupt the sound palette when it might become too comfortable. Greenwood re-employed its disquieting ambience for his soundtrack to 2007's *There Will Be Blood*, while his string arrangements for 'How to Disappear Completely' took inspiration from avant-garde composer Krzysztof Penderecki, whom he had long admired.

Yorke himself didn't think it all that radical. *Select* magazine concurred, with the waspish 'What do they want for sounding like Aphex Twin circa 1993, a medal?' *MOJO* found it disappointing and hoped 'that some trump cards are being saved for later'.

A Bowie-worthy artistic reinvention, then, memorably delivered in Stanley Donwood's artwork of forbidding icy mountains – as impenetrable as some critics found the content. But that's not all. Appearing at the tipping point of the new millennium, *Kid A* was one of the earliest releases by a significant artist in the digital age, when online blogs and message boards provided instant commentary, as opposed to the traditional delay between release and printed review.

Kidding A-round: Oxford's finest get serious

Radiohead offered fans the chance to pre-purchase and stream the album using an iBlip player, via which they could also access a string of enigmatic video clips created by Donwood; despite a leak on Napster, it resulted in 400,000 streams. Commercial suicide? Hardly: it debuted on *Billboard* at No.1, *Time* magazine calling it 'the weirdest album to sell a million records'. In a way not seen before, but which anticipated a trend to come, Radiohead had made their album release a pop-cultural 'moment'. The title of Steven Hyden's 2020 book sums it up: *This Isn't Happening: Radiohead's 'Kid A' and the Beginning of the 21st Century*.

DAFT PUNK REDEFINE DANCE MUSIC – AGAIN

DISCOVERY
DAFT PUNK
2001

With their 1997 debut *Homework*, Parisian duo Daft Punk (Guy-Manuel de Homem-Christo and Thomas Bangalter) took house into retro-future territory. The vocal of hypnotic earworm 'Around the World', whose only lyrics are its title repeated 144 times, was heavily treated with a talk box (made famous by Peter Frampton in the mid-70s). Disco and funk samples abounded – witness the clavinet-like timbres made famous by Stevie Wonder. *Homework*'s infectious signature sounds were swiftly taken up by other artists, reworked in Madonna's 'Music' and Spiller's 'Groovejet', for example. But *Discovery* was to reset the controls for 21st-century dance music.

'When you're a child you don't judge or analyze music,' Bangalter told *Remix* in 2001, summing up the album's exploratory and open-minded aesthetic. 'You just like it because you like it.' So into the blender went Van Halen-indebted guitars ('Aerodynamic'), along with deeply unfashionable soft rock ('Superheroes' samples Barry Manilow's 'Who's Been Sleeping in My Bed', while 'Face to Face' draws on painstakingly chopped-and-looped snippets from ELO and the Alan Parsons Project, among others). They championed eras that had become no-go areas (hello, mid-80s!), burnishing once untouchable tropes till they morphed into warm, euphoric floor-fillers. And if they weren't sampling retro sounds, they were recreating them in the studio, with vintage gear including a Minimoog and classic Roland and Linn drum machines.

From the glossy sheen of its production values, to its muscular beats and vocal treatments, *Discovery* set a whole rack of precedents for 21st-century pop. Soon enough, AOR samples began cropping up in other artists' work – Gary Wright's 'Comin' Apart' in Armand van Helden's 'My My My', for example. 'Harder, Better, Faster, Stronger' is graced with Kraftwerkian *Mensch-Maschine* vocals, which transmute into instrumental solos. 'We put [auto-tuning] in the same category as the wah-wah pedal,' Bangalter told *NME* in 2013. 'It's pleasing to the ear and creates those funky artefacts.' But there's a dry wit at work here too; the ten-minute closer is titled 'Too Long', and surely they didn't intend us to take those baroque keyboard arepeggios ('Superheroes') and that fussy guitar noodling (a *dance* track with a solo?) with a straight face? Pop should be fun, no?

Going *Beyoncé* before Beyoncé, the entire album provided the narrative arc for an accompanying sci-fi anime movie, *Interstella 5555: The 5tory of the 5ecret 5tar 5ystem* (2003), partly screened on the Cartoon Network channel and later

Gallic robots re-set the dance zeitgeist at Coachella, April 2006

INVENTION AND DISSENSION 2000—PRESENT

released alongside 2003's *Daft Club* LP. This two years before YouTube launched. And in a forward-thinking strategy to connect directly with fans, initial copies of the album came with a membership card to join the online Daft Club, via which users could download otherwise-unavailable material. In both cases, it took the world a few years to catch up.

In turn, samples of *Discovery* contributed to an evolution in other genres. Kanye West played his part in electronic dance music's (EDM) growth Stateside (and Daft Punk's rise there) by adapting the hook from 'Harder, Better, Faster, Stronger', adding grandeur and punchiness for 2007's international No.1 'Stronger'. He'd later recruit the duo to work on his acclaimed *Yeezus* (2013).

They sealed their iconic aura with an audacious makeover. The myth, as the pair spun it, was that at 9.09am on 9/9/99, as they were in their studio, Daft House, working on one of the album's tracks, a sampler exploded – triggered by the '9999' bug, they later explained. The incident disfigured the pair so drastically that they were forced to undergo surgery that transformed them into robots. The track was destroyed, so they were forced to start again, now as cyborg composers, with all that that entailed for the music.

Discovery's album artwork includes a shot of the pair as chrome-helmeted automatons, counterintuitively gathered at a grand piano, gleaming gauntlets on its ivory keyboard – spiritual heirs to Kraftwerk's mannequin replicas, which the Düsseldorf quartet first used on stage in 1981, and forerunners of Deadmau5's grinning mau5head. To house-redefining genius and deep pop nous, Daft Punk had now added unforgettable theatre.

'WHILE WE MIGHT HAVE SOME DISCO INFLUENCES, WE DECIDED TO GO FURTHER AND BRING IN ALL THE ELEMENTS OF MUSIC THAT WE LIKED AS CHILDREN.'

THOMAS BANGALTER

Skrillex brings his *Mothership* to the masses

At the opening night of their *Alive* tour at California's Coachella Festival in April 2006, Daft Punk bulldozed the 10,000-plus crowd with a greatest-hits remix from within a pyramid-shaped set – a $300,000 LED lighting set-up that pulsed, throbbed and downright overpowered onlookers. It outrocked most rock bands and set a new benchmark for live electronica in the USA.

Skrillex told the *Guardian* that seeing it was 'like walking into the portal of my destiny'. His 2012–13 *Mothership* tour is a case in point, an immersive live extravaganza for which he donned a motion-capture outfit to manipulate up to eight avatars that were projected onto a 15- x 30-ft structure dubbed 'The Cell'.

Porter Robinson's 2014 *Worlds* tour recruited animators Invisible Light Network to create an extension of the realities conjured up by his music. Incorporating anime, glitch computer-generated art and pixellated forms, and referencing indie video games such as *Torchbearer* and classics such as *Space Harrier*, these epic animated stories played out onstage on a huge bank of LED screens. Ditto the mind-melding mash-up of classic games and *kaiju* that highlighted Deadmau5's live performances and the iterations of his LED-bedecked 3D 'Cube', which has generated progressively more intense graphics, as well as the dazzling visuals emitting from his signature mouse helmet itself.

Hard to believe that EDM artists were once considered incompatible with festivals' dynamics. These state-of-the-art audio-visual blitzes have transformed them into must-see performance experiences.

DIZZYING FAREWELL FROM A BEAT-MAKING GENIUS

DONUTS
J DILLA
2006

Questlove's band the Roots were supporting the Pharcyde one night in 1995, and after playing he popped outside. As the headliners started up, he heard something odd and raced back. 'It was almost like someone drunk was playing drums,' he recalled in his memoir, *Mo' Meta Blues*. 'Or, more so, that a drunk, brilliant four-year-old had been allowed to program the kick pattern.' It happened again when he heard the Slum Village album *Fantastic, Vol.1*, and by now hip-hop front-runners such as D'Angelo and A Tribe Called Quest's Q-Tip were hearing it too. It hit them all like an epiphany: 'There wasn't a sound there,' Questlove marvelled, 'and then, suddenly, there was one.' The alchemist of that sound was J Dilla.

What became *Donuts* started as a calling card – sketches of beats for labels or artists, potential clients. The palette draws deeply on soul music samples, but fractured and redefined, as if seen through a prism. In short, *Donuts* might involve a spot of aural recalibration. Hear it once and the fragmentary sound collages, hip-hop *musique concrète*, could sound chaotic – bitty too, with running times rarely topping 90 seconds. Hear it again and patterns and playful connections start seeping through.

Take the opener 'Donuts (Outro)', a scatological sample and his name stuttering over a creamy backing, a whisker over 10 seconds long. But it's followed by 'Workinonit', which sounds nothing like it, cross-cut with wildly diverse samples (and featuring the siren that crops up across the album, Dilla's aural watermark to remind producers who'd made the track). You'd struggle to call it, or any other track here, a song as such, yet somehow there's musical coherence to it. Plus, Dilla loved errors like other people love guitar solos. 'When I heard mistakes in records it was exciting for me,' he told *Scratch Magazine*, describing it as 'a compilation of the stuff that I thought was a little too much for the MCs'.

Dilla was a sick man; he mostly edited *Donuts* in hospital. It was released on his 32nd birthday, 7 February 2006, and three days later he was dead. You don't need to know that to appreciate this album's out-of-the-box approach to sound manipulation. But if you do, perhaps think of it more as an extraordinary artist's raging against the dying of the light. In *Mo' Meta Blues*, Questlove asserted that it 'made people rethink some of their basic assumptions about music, and not just hip-hop but all recorded music'. Quite the epitaph.

Killer Dilla

PHANTASMAGORIC RAP LANDMARK

MY BEAUTIFUL DARK TWISTED FANTASY
KANYE WEST
2010

MBDTF is a concept album about celebrity, its head-messing highs and soul-destroying lows. En route, its creator revisits past Kanyes, from the sampled soul music that enriched his debut to the open-heart confessions and auto-tuned vocals of *808s & Heartbreak* (2008) and the baroque extravagance of *Late Registration* (2005). Perhaps *Graduation* (2007) was the closest parallel, in its conflation of genres and maximal scale.

It's an aural overload: sample-heavy, zeitgeist-scrutinizing and impossible to take in at the first listen. Into the mix goes prog-rock – an apt complement to the set's outsized grandiosity (encapsulated in that unwieldy title), with snippets from the likes of King Crimson and Mike Oldfield. At its core is Kanye West's voice, but it's only one of them. Guests duet, back and blend with him throughout, as if the things he's trying to convey need multiple tongues. And even when he's singing solo, he often warps the sound with effects.

The bulk of the recording took place in Honolulu's Avex recording studios, which he block-booked, inviting along a cross-genre spectrum of artists – ranging from Drake to Elton John via Rihanna, RZA and Jay-Z – for creative collaboration at what was subsequently dubbed a 'rap camp'. He had a trio of session rooms and moved between them as and when inspiration flagged.

Maybe it took all that to convey the mixed-up state of mind of a cultural icon whose mental stability was cause for public debate. Not least after he notoriously interrupted Taylor Swift's acceptance speech at MTV's Video Music Awards in 2009 to inform her that her Best Female Video gong was rightfully Beyoncé's, prompting a deluge of scorn, including the label 'jackass' from President Barack Obama. The collapse of his relationship with model Amber Rose provided more trauma. In retrospect, those nods to his past glories were a reminder of what his audience had loved about him, an oblique plea for them to stick with him.

West alternates between cocksure aggressor and self-flagellator, narcissist and nihilist, especially in 'Blame Game' (which loops a sample from Aphex Twin's 'Avril 14th') and 'Runaway'. He's implicit among the 'douchebags' he toasts in the latter. And in the former, a confident persona underpinned by John Legend's so-smooth vocal breaks down into utter heartbreak. We glimpse the fallible and vulnerable figure hidden behind West's *Wizard of Oz* curtain.

He takes savage delight in flipping over fame, love and celebrity to show their darker underbellies. 'Monster' parodies his public enemy profile (and features a raga-tinged verse from Nicki Minaj, so brilliant that West half-considered pulling it). Its grand guignol video picked up on the mixture of braggadocio and fallibility

Red star: Kanye at the 2010 MTV VMAs, sporting Louis Vuitton Dons

in the lyrics, not least with its plentiful corpses – lingeried and hanged from chains, propped up on his bed and a feast for zombies. It recalls George Condo's garish artwork, featuring a surreal gallery of grotesques: the main cover shows a nightmarish West straddled by a female phoenix; both are nude and wear smiles that might become bites.

'Power' swings violently from assertive bravado and counterpunches at the critics to an outro hinting at suicide, its sample of King Crimson's '21st Century Schizoid Man' a neat fit both musically and thematically. On the penultimate 'Lost in the World', Justin 'Bon Iver' Vernon reprises his disarmingly beautiful 'Woods', auto-tuned vocals locked in poignant harmony, which breaks unexpectedly into a *cri de coeur* of crashing beats and tribal rhythms. But it leads to an outro of little consolation, an edit of Gil Scott-Heron's 'Comment #1' – wherein the poet decries the myth of the American Dream and flags up street-level desperation of Black citizens, themes still painfully pertinent in West's 2010. Intriguingly, it retains the small, scattered applause of Heron's original version, which might be a humorous, or ironic, reaction to the album we've just heard.

MBDTF remains a landmark in 21st-century pop culture. Among those who have sampled it, perhaps the most notable is Kendrick Lamar, whose 'A Little Appalled' rhymed over a beat from *MBDTF*'s 'So Appalled'; Lamar admired its use of samples that other hip-hop artists would have swerved. Moreover, West teased some of the album's tracks on his G.O.O.D. Friday free-release sessions, building a buzz for an album that was already one of the era's most-anticipated, a strategy that helped lay the ground for similar moves by the likes of Timbaland.

Perhaps its greatest influence was on Kanye West, who presents himself here as a cultural lodestar for the times. With *MBDTF*, he became the subject of his own art – territory that *Yeezus* (2013) and *The Life of Pablo* (2016) continued to explore.

'IT WAS A BACKHANDED APOLOGY. IT WAS LIKE, ALL THESE RAPS, ALL THESE SONIC ACROBATICS. I WAS LIKE: "LET ME SHOW YOU GUYS WHAT I CAN DO..."'

KANYE WEST

DEEP DIGGING, BROAD THINKING: THE RISE OF ART RAP

Art rockers had been around at least since David Bowie and Roxy Music. But at the turn of the 21st century, a rap equivalent took root. 'I started wondering why they had a genre where they can do whatever the fuck they want to do, and rappers are scorned if they don't have enough machismo,' reflected Open Mike Eagle to *LA Weekly* in the year of Kanye West's *MBDTF*'s release.

One crucial progenitor was Freedom Fellowship, the LA rap quartet who deftly incorporated jazz rhythms in the 1990s, and whom art rapper R.A.P. Ferreira cited as his 'Mount Rushmore'. 'We improvise and play off of each other's words and sounds – like jazz musicians do,' the group's Mikah 9 told *LA Weekly* in 1993, 'liberating rap from its R&B/funk structures – that 4/4 (time) prison.'

So-called 'art rap' is defiantly leftfield, embracing tropes that mainstream rap eschews, with no eye to the commercial main prize. Typical features include innovative production, assumption of characters in narrative, atypical song forms heavy with allusion and double meaning, and cross-cultural references – making *MBDTF* sound like art rap writ maximally large. Some artists express that quest for originality with deep knowledge of literary tradition and with renewed emphasis on Black identity. 'These are the smartest, most well-informed, best orators of their generation,' writer and podcaster Nate LeBlanc told complex.com's Shawn Setaro in 2020. One key figure associated with the genre, Elucid, was raised in the Pentecostal Church and brings the cadences and flow of a preacher's delivery to play in his rhymes.

Broad politics frequently finds focus in personal tales. On *Brick Body Kids Still Daydream* (2017), Open Mike Eagle explores the demolition of the Robert Taylor Homes housing project on Chicago's South Side, exploding familiar clichés about their supposed soullessness, its anger leavened with compassion and wit.

THE FIRST APP-ALBUM

BIOPHILIA
BJÖRK
2011

With her eighth album, the relentlessly innovative Björk produced a convention-trashing multimedia experience. A hybrid audio-visual app/concept album that explores humanity's affinity with the natural world and the universe. In 2014, it became the first of its kind to appear in New York's Museum of Modern Art.

The music itself is some of the most affecting she has created, from the disarming melodies of 'Solstice' and 'Virus' to the enveloping choral arrangements and forlorn brass of 'Cosmogony'. The songs' form also reflects their theme in some way: on 'Moon', musical motifs repeat in cycles, while the contrapuntal structure of 'Solstice' reflects the movements of the planets in space, and Earth's rotation around its axis.

Fittingly for a project that attempts to address the inexpressible mystery and majesty of the bits of existence that aren't us, Björk commissioned bespoke instruments, including the gameleste (a MIDI-triggered hybrid of a gamelan's metal bars in a celeste's casing) that sprinkles music-box tonalities across 'Crystalline' and 'Virus'. 'Solstice' incorporates software-controlled 'gravity harps', their strings sounded by the movement of pendulums, while a sharpsichord, or pin barrel harp, appears on 'Sacrifice', its notes struck by studs on a rotating cylinder.

Biophilia's ten tracks are each paired with an interactive app for iPad and iPhone, their imagery inspired by gaming. 'In a way, every app is a visualization of the song,' Björk explained to *Drowned in Sound* in 2011. 'You are inside the song... I wanted it to be that you could see the sounds.' Its core 'mother app' – representing the song 'Cosmogony' – appears as a galaxy turning in the blackness of space, with each song a glowing star. Click on one, and users can hear its music, but each app also opens a world of additional features, such as visual games, or allows users to manipulate its elements, producer-like, for an on-the-spot remix. 'Virus' positions the user as a cell under attack, while 'Crystalline' invites you to choose the pathway via which a crystal falls through a series of tunnels, morphing in structure according to the course you choose for it and the additional crystals you pick up en route. But rather like Alice tumbling down a rabbit hole into Wonderland, further delights await in each app – access the score and lyrics, or watch as an animation enacts the movements of a song's constituent parts as it plays.

A multifaceted audio-visual cosmos orbiting around a hard educational core? A decade on, *Biophilia* is still without equal.

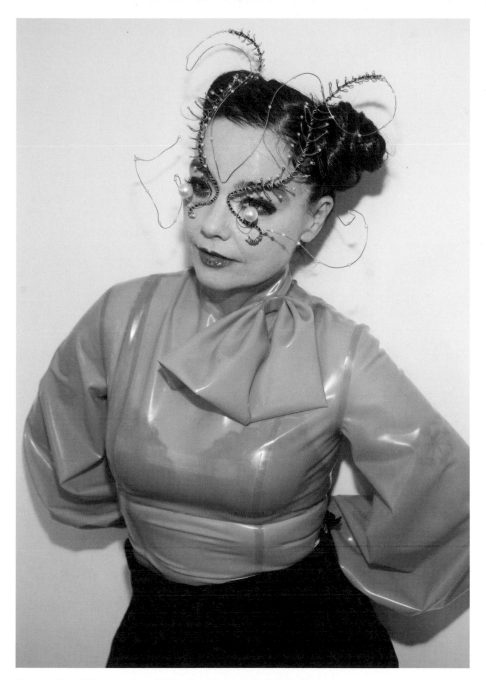

The natural look: Björk wears a James T. Merry headpiece and a top by Syren Latex

INVENTION AND DISSENSION 2000–PRESENT

INDUSTRY-BAMBOOZLING SURPRISE-RELEASE VISUAL ALBUM

BEYONCÉ
BEYONCÉ
2013

Beyoncé in her imperial phase matched huge popularity to unquenchable ambition, knuckle-down drive and a sublime disregard for convention. With the second decade of the 21st century, her music-making took on a more radical, even subversive edge.

On 13 December, while still engaged with her *Mrs. Carter Show* world tour, she dropped her fifth, eponymous album on iTunes, a deeply personal set that gave listeners a front-row seat at Beyoncéworld. We get a time-machine trip back to her youthful flop with Girls Tyme on *Star Search* in '***Flawless', along with a TED talk about feminism and sisterhood from Nigerian author Chimamanda Ngozi Adichie. There are reflections on motherhood: 'Blue' features her daughter Blue Ivy on giggles, while the video for 'Grown Woman' includes clips of herself in younger incarnations. And – over the course of a steamy septet of tracks – explicit sex. Plenty of it, and all with one man: her husband, Jay-Z. Lascivious sex on the back seat of a limo ('Partition') – chauffeur-driven, of course; sex all over the house on 'Drunk in Love', on which the two trade heated imagery. (A lusty paean to sex *within* marriage? How off-the-wall is that?)

Throughout, her vocals are nuanced and focused, taking in spoken half-raps over beats, Arabic-inflected scales, ecstatic whoops, feisty in-your-face assertion – effortlessly appropriating the bravado long synonymous with male rappers – close-mic breathiness, ear-catching ad-libs. An artist totally in control, portraying a woman deliriously losing it.

The music was just part of the multimedia package, though. *Beyoncé* was a 'visual album', 14 music tracks in tandem with 17 short films – cutting-edge works by the likes of Hype Williams (whose videos had helped cement Missy Elliott's image the previous decade) and Jonas Åkerlund, whose hefty CV jumps from works as diverse as Prodigy's 'Smack My Bitch Up' to Lady Gaga via Madonna's 'Ray of Light' via Rammstein.

Beyoncé had laid the groundwork for her solo success with R&B trio Destiny's Child, but here she's mix-and-matching genres and stretching tracks out via interludes and suite-style forms. Perhaps that's a tribute to the 40-plus collaborators, including prime movers Drake and Frank Ocean – not to mention her husband. And also the various producers on board, including Pharrell Williams, Timbaland and the hitherto little-known Boots, who reported that he

He *did* put a ring on it. Bey triumphs at the 2013 Super Bowl XLVII Halftime Show

INVENTION AND DISSENSION 2000—PRESENT

produced 85 per cent of the album and whose Aphex Twin-like 'Ghost' informed the album's 'Haunted'.

Experimentation and textural diversity are high on the agenda, three-minute pop tunes less so, to the extent that no obvious singles leap out (although the extracted 'Drunk in Love' made *Billboard* No.2). *Beyoncé* delights in wrong-footing and defying expectations of what she, or contemporary pop, should be. Her sister Solange's contemporary explorations may have been an influence – her self-curated *Saint Heron* compilation, released shortly before *Beyoncé*, offered variations on fresh, minimalist alt-R&B.

By 2013, avant-gardists such as Björk and Radiohead had pushed against the expectations surrounding an album, in terms of presentation, manner of release and even how much to pay for it – if anything. Beyoncé added her own twist. Industry convention has it that artists offer taster singles, then deliver the parent album and tour to support them. With Beyoncé, there were no appetite-whetting videos, tracks or even leaks. Songs that had already appeared that year in TV commercials either weren't on the album at all ('Standing on the Sun', written by Sia, for H&M) or appeared as a visual only ('Grown Woman', for Pepsi, a bonus video cut here). She'd done it all about-face: world tour, during which an album unexpectedly drops, followed by the singles.

The album's unexpected release became *the* pop happening of its time, and an intense talking point in itself. Social media went ballistic, fans scrabbling to hear the set and share their euphoria – effectively pitching in to help market the album for her. Within three hours, 80,000 fans had listened to it. 'Don't talk to me today,' tweeted Katy Perry on the day of its release, 'unless it's about @Beyonce.'

Beyoncé revisited the surprise release with 2016's *Lemonade*. Another visual album, though this time built around a no-holds-barred dissection of troubles in her country and her own marriage, which gave the album's exclusive streaming on Tidal – then owned by her husband, Jay-Z – extra grit and piquancy. But the game-changing proper kicked off with *Beyoncé*.

'I DIDN'T WANT TO RELEASE MY MUSIC THE WAY I'VE DONE IT. I AM BORED WITH THAT. '

BEYONCÉ

Channel yellow: Frank Ocean at the 2013 Grammys

Out-of-the-blue albums became something of a Beyoncé trademark. She did it again in 2018 with *Everything is Love*, a joint release with husband Jay-Z that quietly appeared on Tidal's music library – which he owned. But the 'drop release' had been around for a while.

David Bowie abruptly returned after years of lying low with 'Where Are We Now?', which hit iTunes on 8 January 2013 – his 66th birthday. 'He's come back with more of a media storm than any other artist has produced in recent years,' *Music Week* editor Tim Ingham told the *Guardian* admiringly.

Why do it? Surely it flies in the face of conventional industry practices – press interviews and appetizers to hype up anticipation before an album explodes into the world? Artists' motivations are likely as unique as their music. Frank Ocean's breakthrough *channel ORANGE* (2012) was surprise released for a transparent reason: it dropped a week ahead of its scheduled date to forestall leaks, a tactic Kanye West and Jay-Z had employed with 2011's *Watch the Throne*. Ocean repeated this by debuting the acclaimed *Blonde* without warning on 20 August 2016. This just a day after his video album *Endless* appeared exclusively as a visual stream on Apple Music. It received less effusive reviews, but fulfilled his Def Jam contract.

Blonde made No.1 in seven countries. Ocean had swapped a deal that gave him 14 per cent on royalties and publishing for one that gave him 70 per cent. And flipped the finger at his old label into the bargain.

FLUX AND FLOW

TO PIMP A BUTTERFLY
KENDRICK LAMAR
2015

Lamar's no-bullshit major-label debut *good kid, m.A.A.d city* (2012) chronicled his fraught upbringing in Compton and how it shaped him. But this follow-up sent shockwaves through hip-hop and beyond.

To Pimp a Butterfly performs an unflinching biopsy of contemporary US society and Lamar himself: what it means to be Black, and its uplifting possibilities; ownership of responsibility (including himself, as a figurehead); seeking inspiration in Black history.

His deft wordplay regularly astonishes, with layers of meaning ripe for unpicking. For the Roots' Questlove, Lamar embodies the complete MC, piling up tiers of double or triple entendres: 'He is what hip hop is about... [trying to work out] if he's being ironic here, or if he's a character here, or the fact that he's using multiple voices.' 'Wesley's Theory' addresses exploitation by the music industry ('pimping' talent), and the legal and moral pitfalls of stellar financial success for Black entertainers not equipped for it and who have shucked off their community. The desperate 'u' digs deep into Lamar's own self-doubts ('all my insecurities and selfishness and letdowns', he told *Rolling Stone*), with the funky, Isley-Brothers-sampling 'i' as its positive complement – a one-two punch delving into the complex issue of self-love in Black artists, for whom swagger, vanity and satire can also represent political defiance against everyday racist oppression. The 12-minute finale 'Mortal Man', partly informed by a visit to Nelson Mandela's Robben Island cell, incorporates a far-reaching dialogue on the Black condition crafted between Lamar and (via a 1994 interview) the late Tupac Shakur.

As a free-flowing state-of-the-Black-union address, *TPAB* has an antecedent in Marvin Gaye's 1971 opus *What's Going On*, and jazz (cut here with G-funk and monologues) provides background texture in both. Saxophonist Kamasi Washington is the musical director, appearing alongside pianist Robert Glasper and bassist extraordinaire Thundercat among other luminaries. 'We are as fluent in J Dilla and Dr Dre as we are in Mingus and Coltrane,' Washington affirms.

In 'Alright' – also informed by that South African trip – Lamar penned a luminous, affirmative statement in the face of adversity and adverse temptations, set to a Pharrell-helmed bounce. Taken up at Black Lives Matter protests, its chorus became a celebratory and defiant anthem. 'The gospel of social movements has many books,' social activist Brittany Packnett stated in the 2021 documentary series *Hip Hop: The Songs That Shook America*. 'To lament how things are right now, that's *What's Going On*. To empower us to be ready for the fight, that's "Fight the Power". To help us preserve our hope, that's "Alright".'

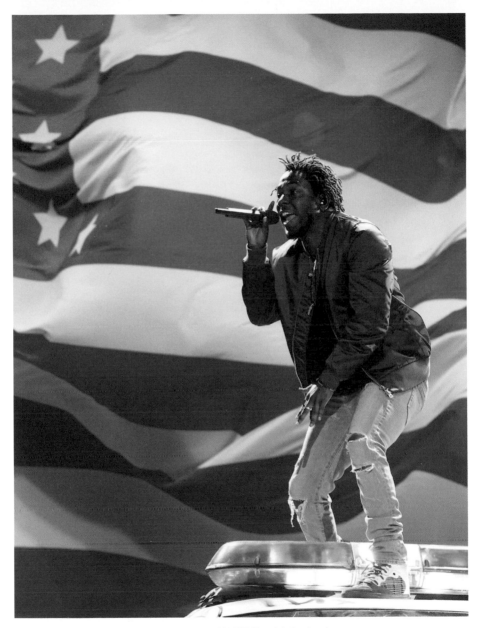

Disunited States: Kendrick Lamar takes a stand at the 2015 BET Awards in Los Angeles

BLACK LIVES MATTER

In early 2012, black teenager Trayvon Martin was shot dead. His murderer's acquittal in July the following year saw social media platforms ablaze with a new hashtag: #BlackLivesMatter. Rising concern at excessive force against Black and mixed-race individuals by police Stateside inspired a breakout of headline-grabbing protests and a re-energization of the civil rights movement. BLM's resonance plays out from street to sporting arena: in September 2016, NFL star Colin Kaepernick of the San Francisco 49ers became the first sportsperson to 'take a knee' during the national anthem, a gesture reflecting the racial inequality that continues to dog US society, and the cost of police brutality in terms of Black lives lost. The move was taken up by other sportspeople, including Premier League and international footballers.

Pop reflected the troubled times. Beyoncé's 'Formation' (2016) was a flat-out celebration of Black pride and a vignette of racial disparities in 21st-century America. The video finds Queen Bey reclining on a slowly submerging police car – a nod to the floods in New Orleans that disproportionately affected citizens of colour – with the plea 'Stop Shooting Us' graffitied on a wall. At that year's Super Bowl 50 in San Francisco, she performed the track alongside dancers decked out like bereted Black Panthers – albeit in leather hot pants. (The Panthers were formed in neighbouring Oakland.) Afterwards, her troupe posed with fists raised in Black Power salutes, à la Tommie Smith and John Carlos at the 1968 Mexico Olympics. They also held up a card reading 'Justice for Mario Woods', a Black man killed in a hail of bullets by police officers in San Francisco the previous December. Janelle Monáe's 'Hell You Talmbout' runs through a roll call of Black youth gunned down by policemen, including Trayvon Martin, Michael Brown and Emmett Till – a 14-year-old Mississippian lynched in 1955 for allegedly disrespecting a white woman.

The death of George Floyd – suffocated by a Minneapolis policeman kneeling on his neck and back for more than nine minutes – crystallized the issue.

Running for dear life: Childish Gambino's compelling video for 'This is America'

NWA's 'Fuck tha Police' saw an increase in streaming of nearly 300 per cent in its wake, while H.E.R.'s track 'I Can't Breathe' – George Floyd's last words – won a Grammy for Song of the Year.

No surprise that pop music and imagery took a visceral turn. Take Childish Gambino's 'This is America'; the unsettling video references gun violence in a string of disturbing scenes, including one in which a choir is brutally mown down – likely a reference to a 2015 massacre in a Black church in Charleston, South Carolina, though it surely also evoked the Ku Klux Klan's bombing of a Black church in Birmingham, Alabama, in 1963, in which four young girls died. It climaxes with the bare-chested singer, wide-eyed, racing straight towards the camera in terrified flight from white pursuers.

Beyoncé's sister Solange summed it all up in her acclaimed 2016 album, a nuanced snapshot of what it means to be young and Black in America right now. Its title evoked Jim Crow-era segregation of Black customers, and was a spiritual brother to Langston Hughes's 1926 poem 'I, Too, Sing America' and Bob Dylan's 'The Lonesome Death of Hattie Carroll': *A Seat at the Table*.

INVENTION AND DISSENSION 2000–PRESENT

GRIME GETS POLITICAL

STORMZY AT THE BRITS
STORMZY
2018

He'd had Top 40 hits since 2015, and in March 2017 *Gang Signs & Prayer* debuted at No.1 in the UK. But political engagement dovetails with Stormzy's creative output, and in June 2017, he contributed to a charity cover of 'Bridge Over Troubled Water' for the victims of the horrific conflagration that consumed the Grenfell tower block in Tower Hamlets, leaving 71 dead and hundreds homeless. The same month, on Glastonbury's Other Stage, he called out the authorities over the tragedy.

Stormzy railed against the government at that year's Brit Awards, and bad-mouthed UK Prime Minister Theresa May at an awards ceremony. And he was far from done. Closing out the 2018 Brits (he was named Best British Male Solo Artist), spotlit as rain cascaded onto his bare skin, he used the primetime show-closing spot to deliver a pointed freestyle against May for the lethargic response to the Grenfell disaster: 'Yo, Theresa May, where's that money for Grenfell? What you thought we just forgot about Grenfell?' Then, a broader anti-establishment attack: 'You criminals, and you got the cheek to call us savages. You should do some jail time you should pay some damages, we should burn your house down and see if you can manage this.' That blistering call-out got a hasty response from the government the following morning, but also praise from Labour's leader Jeremy Corbyn – his star then in the ascendant.

The following year, Stormzy became the first Black British headliner on Glastonbury's Pyramid stage. His expansive set incorporated dance troupe Black Ballet, guests including Coldplay's Chris Martin, and another dig at the establishment, getting the crowd to chant a profanity-packed anti-government swipe from his No.1 'Vossi Bop'. His costume was just as provocative: a black stab-proof vest bearing the Union Jack, referencing the UK's knife-crime epidemic and attendant gang violence. Its designer? Shadowy graffiti artist Banksy – something that, reportedly, Stormzy was unaware of (he tweeted that he was 'absolutely f****** speechless' at the news).

'I don't want this to be about me,' he told the BBC after that fiery 2018 Brits set. 'It's not about me – it's about Grenfell and it's about all the things I said in that lyric. This is bigger than me.' He's since used his cultural clout to push through meaningful change, partnering his #Merky charity with HSBC to provide scholarships to help fund Black and mixed-race students to study at Cambridge University, and launching a publishing imprint within Random House for young writers. Backing up that searing socio-political comment with meaningful action.

Point made: Stormzy at the 2018 Brits

INVENTION AND DISSENSION 2000–PRESENT

#METOO

The term 'me too' was coined in 2006 by activist Tarana Burke on MySpace, to denote sexual harassment, especially that which targets women of colour, and spread the word that such victims are not alone. (Latest figures suggest that one in four women in the USA have suffered rape, or attempted rape, while revenge porn affects some 1 in 12 Stateside.*) But it became headline news in 2017 when actress Alyssa Milano suggested victims of abuse write #MeToo on social media platforms, to flag up the scale of the issue. Within 24 hours, 4.7 million users had done just that on Facebook alone.

In 2015, Lady Gaga (who had herself been raped as a teenager) penned an anthem to unite victims of abuse in 'Till it Happens to You', its message crystallized when she performed it at the 2016 Oscars, surrounded by 50 survivors of abuse, sporting messages such as 'not your fault'. The following year, Kesha's 'Praying' was widely interpreted as a commentary on her alleged abuse by former producer Dr Luke, though the lyric names no names.

The drive for self-empowerment has echoes elsewhere in the music industry. Pop queen Taylor Swift dramatically rebounded from the blow of having the rights to her back catalogue sold by Scott Borchetta – head of her former label, Big Machine – to Scooter Braun – then manager of her sometime sparring partner Kanye West. In response she began note-for-note 'Taylor's Version' re-recordings of her albums to replace the originals, reclaiming ownership of her own music a track at a time. *Red (Taylor's Version)* was released in November 2021.

Swift and her sister pop-luminaries such as Beyoncé are not only inspirational artists, but their own bosses too. They're building on the straight-talking rap of Queen Latifah, and Janet Jackson's artistic rebirth as expressed through *Control* (1986) and the socially engaged *Rhythm Nation 1814* (1989). As with Jackson, Beyoncé's vault from from pop princess to politically engaged artist kicked in after breaking with her own manager/father. Lady Gaga's stellar success is testament to titanic self-belief.

'Till it Happens to you'. And you. And #MeToo. Lady Gaga and sister victims stand tall at the 2016 Oscars

Like David Bowie as Ziggy Stardust, she sprang forth fully formed as a self-declared star, a claim that the mega-selling *The Fame* (2008) duly reinforced.

Few high-profile contemporary female artists have crashed as heavily as Britney Spears. Her father's controversial conservatorship (revoked in November 2021) may have exacerbated her decline – Spears alleged that she'd been forced to perform against her will – but the media played its part too. Who among her male peers would have been so aggressively quizzed about his virginity or parenting skills? Or have his rehab history relentlessly probed, as veteran chat-show host David Letterman did with Lindsay Lohan? Similar double standards saw Janet Jackson's career nosedive after her infamous 'wardrobe malfunction' at the 2004 Super Bowl, while that of Justin Timberlake, the perpetrator, sailed on. Proof positive of the need for parity and collective support that the #MeToo movement is pushing so hard to achieve.

* Source: metoomvmt.org

GLOSSARY

Analogue recording: The process of capturing sound so as to document all of its possible frequencies.

Atonality: Music that has no definite keys, or – put another way – has multiple possibilities. (Compare with **Tonality**.)

Attack: The build-up of a note, from absolute silence to its peak level.

Chromaticism: The introduction of notes outside the primary key of a composition.

Compressor: An audio tool that reduces the dynamic range of a sound – i.e., the difference between its quietest and loudest parts.

Cubism: Pioneered by Pablo Picasso and George Braque, this radical artistic approach sought to convey multiple viewpoints of a subject simultaneously.

Dadaism: An avant-garde European artistic movement that began in around 1915 and was characterized by satire, absurdity and nonsense.

Digital recording: The translation of sound into numbers as an approximation of what the listener hears.

Equalizer: An audio filter used to alter the balance of aural frequencies in a recording. Also known as an 'EQ'.

Expressionism: Starting in the late 19th century, this artistic movement sought to express subjective inner feelings and emotions rather than document objective external realities.

Fauvism: Short-lived artistic style, based in Paris, typified by non-naturalistic, expressionistic use of colour.

Minimalism: A term applied broadly to music that features relatively few component parts, little melodic or harmonic variation and is often characterized by repetition.

Multi-tracking: The process of layering recorded parts over each other.

Neorealism: In film, a movement initiated in Italy typified by stories of working-class life. Its heyday lasted from the early 1940s for around a decade.

Phasing: In composition, the effect created when two identical parts are played steadily on two different sources (e.g. instruments or playback devices such as tape recorders) that gradually shift out of unison. The term is also applied to a musical effect (created by an electronic sound processor known as a 'phaser') that adds a sweeping quality to an audio signal by varying its peaks and troughs over time.

Phoneme: The smallest possible unit of sound in a word – e.g. 'b' and 'd' in 'bad'.

Pianism: The artistry and craft of piano playing.

Polyrhythm: The use of multiple, contrasting rhythms played at the same time.

Polytonality: The simultaneous use of several keys (or 'tonalities') in a musical piece.

Readymades: Found objects (typically mass-produced and commercially available) that are presented as art. The term was coined by Marcel Duchamp and is most famously associated with his 1917 work *Fountain* (a urinal).

Sampling: The technique of capturing and re-using recorded sound in a new musical composition. This may also involve treating the sample using production tools.

Serialism: Primarily developed by Arnold Schoenberg, this method of musical composition uses a set series (or 'row') of notes as the basis for a work. The series must be worked through, in order, before repeating it, although the composer can introduce variation by inverting, or reversing the row, for example.

Sine wave: The fundamental waveform from which other waveforms may be generated. It is represented on a graph as an 's'-shaped wave that oscillates above and below a horizontal line representing zero.

Surrealism: An early 20th-century artistic movement that took inspiration from irrationality, the unconscious and dream imagery.

Syncopation: Emphasis on the 'off' beats in a musical bar – i.e., those that don't fall on the main beat and aren't usually stressed. In a regular bar of four beats, the main beats are 1 and 3 and the 'off beats' are beats 2 and 4.

Tonality: 1. Music that revolves around a definite key, known as the 'tonic'. Typically, the composition will gravitate away from the tonic during the course of the work, but return to it at the end, implying a sense of resolution and closure. (Compare with **Atonality**.) 2. The tonal quality, or character, of a piece of music.

- Albertine, Viv (2014), *Clothes Clothes Clothes Music Music Music Boys Boys Boys*, Faber & Faber

- Anderson, Darran (2019), *Histoire de Melody Nelson*, Bloomsbury

- Barfe, Louis (2005 edition), *Where Have all the Good Times Gone? The Rise and Fall of the Record Industry*, Atlantic Books

- Brend, Mark (2012), *The Sound of Tomorrow: How Electronic Music was Smuggled into the Mainstream*, Bloomsbury

- Busy, Pascal (2001), *Kraftwerk: Man, Machine and Music*, SAF Publishing

- Chang, Jeff (2007 edition), *Can't Stop, Won't Stop: A History of the Hip-Hop Generation*, Ebury Press

- Davis, Miles with Troupe, Quincy (1990 edition), *Miles: The Autobiography*, Touchstone

- Dunn, Christopher: Brutality Garden (2001), *Tropicália and the Emergence of a Brazilian Counterculture*, University of North Carolina Press

- Easton, M. Laird (ed. and trans. 2011), *Journey to the Abyss: The Diaries of Count Harry Kessler, 1880–1918*, Alfred A. Knopf

- Ferguson, Jordan (2014), *Donuts*, Bloomsbury

- Guralnick, Peter (1999 edition), *Last Train to Memphis: The Rise of Elvis Presley*, Abacus

- Holiday, Billie with Dufty, William (1984 edition), *Lady Sings the Blues: The Searing Autobiography of an American Musical Legend*, Penguin

- Kurlansky, Mark (2013), *Ready for a Brand New Beat: How 'Dancing in the Street' Became the Anthem for a Changing America*, Riverhead Books

- MacDonald, Bruno (2020), *666 Metal Songs to Make You Bang Your Head Until You Die: A Guide to the Monsters of Rock and Metal*, Laurence King

- Murray, Charles Shaar (1989), *Crosstown Traffic: Jimi Hendrix and Post-War Pop*, Faber & Faber

- Phillips, Stephanie (2021), *Why Solange Matters*, Faber & Faber

- Prendergrass, Mark (2003 edition), *The Ambient Century: From Mahler to Moby – The Evolution of Sound in the Electronic Age*, Bloomsbury

- Reynolds, Simon (2013 edition), *Energy Flash: A Journey Through Rave Music and Dance Culture*, Faber & Faber

- Roberts, Martin (2019), *Fantasma*, Bloomsbury

- Ross, Alex (2011 edition), *Listen to This*, Fourth Estate

- Ross, Alex (2008 edition), *The Rest is Noise: Listening to the Twentieth Century*, Fourth Estate

- Savage, Jon (2015), *1966: The Year the Decade Exploded*, Faber & Faber

- Savage, Jon (1991), *England's Dreaming: Sex Pistols and Punk Rock*, Faber & Faber

- Shapiro, Peter (2020 edition), *Turn the Beat Around: The Secret History of Disco*, Faber & Faber

- Thomson, Ahmir 'Questlove' with Greenman, Ben (2013), *Mo' Meta Blues: The World According to Questlove*, Grand Central Publishing

- Toop, David (2001 edition), *Ocean of Sound: Aether Talk, Ambient Sound and Imaginary Worlds*, Serpent's Tail

- Trynka, Paul (2013 edition), *Starman: David Bowie – The Definitive Biography*, Sphere

- Veloso, Caetano (2003 edition), *Tropical Truth: A Story of Music and Revolution in Brazil*, Bloomsbury

- Verlant, Gilles, trans. Knobloch, Paul (2012 edition), *Gainsbourg: The Biography*, TamTam Books

- Wald, Elijah (2009), *How the Beatles Destroyed Rock'n'Roll: An Alternative History of Popular Music*, Oxford University Press

PICTURE CREDITS

The publishers would like to thank all those listed below for permission to reproduce the images featured in this book. Every care has been taken to trace copyright holders. Any copyright holders we have been unable to reach are invited to contact the publishers so that a full acknowledgement may be given in subsequent editions.

6 Santiago Felipe/Getty Images; 9 GAB Archive/ Getty Images; 17 Keystone-France/Getty Images; 21 Heritage Image Partnership Ltd/Alamy; 23 Gilles Petard/Getty Images; 25 Niday Picture Library/Alamy; 27 Glasshouse Images/Alamy; 29 Photo 12/Getty Images; 31 Soundonsound; 33 Michael Ochs Archives/Getty Images; 37 The Museum of Modern Art, New York/Scala, Florence; 39 Allstar Picture Archive Ltd/Alamy; 47 Pictorial Press Ltd/Alamy; 49 Michael Ochs Archives/Getty Images; 51 Herve GLOAGUEN/Getty Images; 53 Effectrode; 55 Michael Ochs Archives/Getty Images; 57 Bill Wagg/Getty Images; 59 PA Images/ Alamy; 61 Pictorial Press Ltd/Alamy; 63 Michael Ochs Archives/Getty Images; 65 Michael Ochs Archives/Getty Images; 67 Alice Ochs/Getty Images; 77 Herve GLOAGUEN/Getty Images; 81 Miro-Medium; 83 Records/Alamy; 85 Collection Christophel/Alamy; 89 Allan Tannenbaum/Getty Images; 91 Wikicommons; 93 Pete Still/Getty Images; 95 Jack Dayman/Getty Images; 97 Jim Britt/Getty Images; 99 DEUTSCH Jean-Claude/ Getty Images; 101 Debi Doss/Getty Images; 103 Leni Sinclair/Getty Images; 105 Echoes/Getty Images; 107 Albumchats; 109 Kraftwerk/Getty Images; 111 David Corio/Getty Images; 113 Charles Steiner/Getty Images; 115 Chris Morphet/Getty Images; 117 Kevin Cummins/Getty Images; 125 Michael Ochs Archives/Getty Images; 127 Donaldson Collection/Getty Images; 131 Roberta Bayley/Getty Images; 133 Pictorial Press Ltd/ Alamy; 135 David Cario/Getty Images; 137 Ebet Roberts/Getty Images; 139 Paul Natkin/Getty Images; 141 Steve Rapport/Getty Images; 143 Ebet Roberts/Getty Images; 145 Paul Natkin/Getty Images; 147 PYMCA/UIG/Getty Images; 149 Lisa Haun/Getty Images; 153 Records/Alamy; 157 dpa picture alliance/Getty Images; 159 Mick Hutson/ Getty Images; 161 Ebet Roberts/Getty Images; 163 Lefse/Post Modern; 173 Bob Berg/Getty Images; 175 Karl Walter/Getty Images; 177 Marco Prosch/ Getty Images; 179 Gregory Bojorquez/Getty Images; 181 Kevin Mazur/Getty Images; 185 Santiago Felipe/Getty Images; 187 Kevin Mazur/ Getty Images; 189 Kevork Djansezian/Getty Images; 191 Christopher Polk/BET; 193 LANDMARK MEDIA/Alamy; 195 Samir Hussein/ Getty Images; 197 REUTERS/Alamy

MUSICQUAKE
AUTHOR ACKNOWLEDGEMENTS

First and foremost, my love and
heartfelt thanks to Andrea and Tomi,
for giving me the space and time to
write this book. Props too to Alice
Graham, who commissioned me, and
Joe Hallsworth, who steered the
manuscript home.

CULTURE QUAKE

A bold new series charting popular
culture's most disruptive, rebellious
and ground breaking works.

ARTQUAKE:
THE MOST DISRUPTIVE WORKS
IN MODERN ART
Susie Hodge

FASHIONQUAKE:
THE MOST DISRUPTIVE MOMENTS
IN FASHION
Caroline Young

FILMQUAKE:
THE MOST DISRUPTIVE FILMS
IN CINEMA
Ian Haydn Smith

MUSICQUAKE:
THE MOST DISRUPTIVE MOMENTS
IN MUSIC
Robert Dimery